BACK ROADS
OF SPAIN

May you have great roads

Duncan Bryce

BACK ROADS
OF SPAIN

DUNCAN GOUGH

Matador
9 De Montfort Mews
Leicester LE1 7FW, UK
Tel: (+44) 116 255 9311 / 9312
Email: books@troubador.co.uk
Web: www.troubador.co.uk/matador

ISBN 978-1848761-421

A Cataloguing-in-Publication (CIP) catalogue record for this book
is available from the British Library.

Matador is an imprint of Troubador Publishing Ltd

Printed in Great Britain by the MPG Books Group, Bodmin and King's Lynn

Contents

My Horse is growing weary.

My horse is growing weary. I am growing weary. Long miles, fallen behind, these have taken a toll. Fingers are numbing, wrists ache and a muscle in my leg threatens to cramp. Though we still match speed to surface there is not that smooth flow, that oneness that desires yet more road to travel. It is time to find an end, juice for 'Veloz', food and bed for me. Dusk is hard upon us, trying to overtake. The nebulous, danger hour, lights look dim as yet, but already the trail and trees are blurring together in the near distance. The 'Hour of Spirits'. Lurking tractors that turn to hedgerow shadow as you prepare yourself, shadow that hides the mud on the road until you are close upon it. Walkers suddenly appear on the verge as if coagulating from the shades of dusk. The way ahead becomes less real; it could go anywhere. Half an hour ago I could catch glimpses of it in the distance, guess its route by telephone poles and the bend of hedges. In full dark you can track it by the twists and turns of oncoming lights, trace coming corners by hot brake lights; not now. The new dampness of dusk sharpens up the days smells; before morning it will lay them down with the dew. A farmer has been cutting silage; moments later I seem to have buried my nose in the moist tilth of a new-ploughed field. That house has a wood-burner, burning sweet apple. Phew! That one has just lit coal that stings with its acridity. Ahead the road rises to a crest outlined in tones of grey. Dropping the reins as we reach the top I coast to a stop at the roadside. A low wide valley opens its arms wide. In its heart a small town. Lights are slowly clicking on and mist rises like moonlight from the wandering course of a river. Dark closes fast about us now. I pat Veloz's tank. "A mile or two and we'll put up." Taking up the reins I clunk us into first and Veloz's heartbeat again lifts to the song of the road that turns us on down the sweeping arms to the valley bottom. That was a journey from my mind, from imagination. But it could have been real. It is certainly filtered from many real experiences.

Burgos and Back.
(2000+ miles in a week on a Moto Guzzi Centauro)

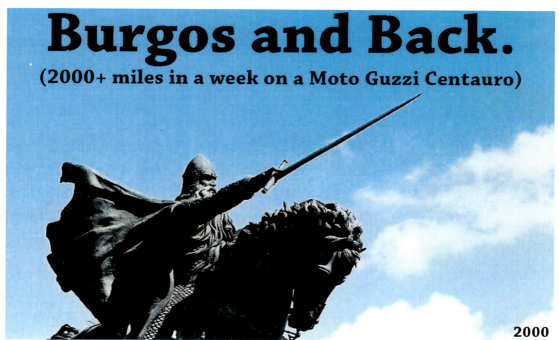

2000

Burgos in Northern Spain. El Cid came from here. As well as being an important site on the pilgrim trail to Santiago de Compostela it has many historic monuments. Anyway, to my story: Three years ago with our climbing affluence we finally managed to plan a 'family' holiday to Spain. During the holiday we visited Burgos and in a shop near the Cathedral my wife saw a rosary that she really fancied. Unfortunately going back the next day to buy it we discovered that it was an 'All Saints' day and the shop was shut. We had to head back to the coast the next day and so in a spirit of selfless sacrifice I vowed 'hand on heart' to return on my motorbike and get the said rosary! Unfortunately this offer was seen in a somewhat cynical light by the rest of my family, and I had to agree to take them all to Glasgow for 3 days in compensation!

The Bike: A V10 Moto Guzzi Centauro. Bought new in Jan 99. 992cc of Italian craft. White Power suspension, Brembo disks; the list goes on… I had always fancied a Moto Guzzi since the days of my youth when I first saw a S7 and couldn't afford it! So with my 25yr old Yamaha XS750 getting a bit passed it, I started to look at Moto Guzzis. The Nevada seemed a bit small and tame and the California a bit too big and laid back for my style and the twisty mountain roads around my home in Aberystwyth. On the other hand the Daytona and 1100 were too uncompromisingly Sports/Racer. The day I sat on a Centauro I knew it was the bike for me. My knees fitted nicely into the tank indents (on the Nevada they were on the rocker covers) and my arms felt comfortable with the handlebars. A nice upright riding position that meant you didn't have to be doing speed to keep your body and wrists comfortable. I asked for a screen and got a Kappa one which really does a good job. I can happily cruise at the ton without arm stretching, on longer distances I normally have a tank bag and can get very comfortable with my chest partially resting on the bag. In severe weather it is possible to really tuck down and look through the screen. Enough blather; to the trip!

Packing:- Oxford tank bag and panniers well stuffed. Binoculars! Daft I know but as an ornithologist I hate being unable to identify that little brown bird in the bush; bird book, camera. Going a thousand miles south necessitated catering for Welsh rain to Spanish heat wave. I have a Frank Thomas fairly bulky Gore-Tex waterproof jacket and Hein Gericke trousers versus Gialli denim jacket and jeans. French and Spanish phrase books. Sleeping bag took up a fair amount of space, one pannier's worth in fact. The basic smalls including light weight but smart clothing for strolling the 'paseo' in Spain.

17th August 2000. Thursday. Aberystwyth to Selborne, Hampshire. 230 miles.

After a fair amount of packing, un-packing and re-packing I finally had the bike loaded. A last minute decision to wear my Gialli denims instead of the waterproof gear; due to the weather appearing to be getting warmer and sunnier necessitated a bit more bag shuffling and re-stuffing but I finally achieved take off. The sun lasted for 30 miles before it started to rain. Having just whipped past a very large timber lorry the initial reaction of 'a few drops won't matter' was quickly revised as in good Welsh fashion it 'chucked it down'! I stopped and got out the waterproof gear and whilst getting into it was covered in spray by the passing timber lorry. Passed him again ten minutes later though, by which time of course it wasn't raining any more! I have over the years of travelling down to Selborne come up with a favourite route. It can be quicker to go from Rhayader down through Builth Wells and Abergavenny to the Severn Bridge and then blast it down the M4. However though the first part of the journey is great, the motorway is motorway and it squares off my tyres! I prefer to go from Rhayader to Leominster and then on to Ledbury, cross the M5, via Birdlip bypass Gloucester and later Cirencester, only hitting the M4 at Swindon. A short dash to Newbury and then past Basingstoke to Alton and finally Selborne. I know this road very well and despite the on-off rain made good time. My bike is named "Veloz"; Spanish for 'swift' and I have a motto of "Veloz y suave" 'swift and smooth'. Knowing the road or reading it well one is always ready to overtake; if it is possible as one comes off the bend. The beauty of the Guzzi is the great stability coupled with the instant acceleration particularly if one is anywhere in the 4-6,000 rpm mark. A twist of the wrist and I am past, drop the throttle back and the shaft/engine breaking neatly drops me back into the gap between cars. Without exceeding speed limits I can keep a respectable 60 mph average across country. One of my favourite aspects of riding the bike is the olfactory input (I wear an open face helmet). It's not just the pleasant smells of elderflower or wood smoke though, it is also an integral part of SAFETY, of anticipating the unexpected. Suddenly smelling fresh mowed grass I cut speed for the next few corners until I find the tractor responsible. Watch out for those thorn cuttings! The fruity aroma of newly slung manure and you take it easy round each corner, a slurry tanker on a plodding tractor is the last thing you want to be running into the back of. Early bed for an early start to catch the Fast Craft from Portsmouth to Cherbourg.

18th August. Friday. Selborne to Derval. Aprox 200 miles on land.

Why is it that once you have gone to all the effort of setting that alarm clock for the crucial 5.30 am call you always wake up at 3, and then at 4 and then half four; in the end you get up at 5 for something to do! A cup of tea (always required in order to start my motor) and I suit up for the short trip down to Portsmouth. Naturally it poured with rain for all the 30 odd miles. Boarding was quick, one always feels a little smug as a biker; you are nearly always put to the front of the queue and get on first. Occasionally this riles some obnoxious git towing an extra large shoebox but thumbs up to them. At least on this P&O Fast Craft they are efficient about tying the bike down with proper padding straps and all. Certain other ferries tend to hand you a greasy bit of rope (if you're lucky), and leave you to find something to tie it off to. Up to the large lounge and grab a good seat. Spotting the eggs and bacon being slung out I had the bright idea of being first in the cue for breakfast. I did have to stand there for a good 20 minutes whilst the little Hitler in charge squared away his butter and marge containers. However I did get my bacon, egg and beans before they had become as stodgy as they would have been for those at the end of the queue! Arriving in France I again put trust in the lack of 'la pluie' despite the lack of 'le soleil', and wore my Gialli's. As I opened her up leaving Cherbourg I thought; 'I'm heading South, the weather has to improve'! The previous year I came to Normandy on the 'Club California' inaugural run so I remembered the combination of long straight stretches of road; which do however dip and rise, often having quite a lot of non-passing stretches, however the French are great drivers in my opinion! They seem to be so much more aware, they do look in their rear view mirrors frequently and spot an upcoming bike. A lot of the time they show they've seen you by pulling over obviously giving you enough space to pass safely without crossing the centre line. I am a fairly cautious rider (still carrying a chunk of steel in one leg from a tractor driver 25 years ago) and never put much trust in the good sense of other road users. Between Valognes and St Sauveur I am passed by a lunatic Triumph (with passenger), he cuts down between the oncoming traffic without waiting for the signal from the cars. I watch him go and I hope for his sake that none of them grabs his baguette for a quick bite and veers out. I start to get the hang of the French wave from other bikers. The low down flick out of two to five fingers (depending on your gloves or lack of them). As I progress the road signs start to sing to me and spark all sort of funny connotations; Bricquebec - 'Bric-a-brac', Barneville Carteret - 'Flintstones', St Lo - 'Sweet chariot', Sartilly - 'Chantilly lace', Granville - 'Open All Hours'. It's funny what keeps you going and alert when riding. I bird watch! I keep an alert eye out for even a fleeting impression. This doesn't mean that I neglect the road, but that I am always looking for a flicker, a wing shape that allows me to identify a kestrel for instance. I am aware of much more that is going on around me than if I just concentrated on the immediate road ahead. The going south doesn't seem to be working on the weather; the rain increases. Do I stop or might it get better? A few miles more and as the road spray builds I give in. Having just hit the dual carriageway at Avranches I stop on the hard shoulder under an overpass to scrabble into my waterproof coat but figure to live with the dampness of the exposed areas of my jeans. One of the nice things about the Centauro is the way in which the cylinders protect your legs to some extent, (no other marque has the transverse twin), tucking in tight behind my screen I cruise through the road spray on the N175 motorway going south from Avranches to Rennes. The Rennes by-pass is well sign posted and I have no trouble picking up the N137 towards Nantes. I am though beginning to realise that I need to re-calibrate my time/distance estimates, I'm thinking of the map in terms of a UK road map where major towns are about 20 miles apart. Not only is this map scale a lot bigger, but in France the towns are 60 or more miles apart! Consequently despite the great roads that tend to mean high average speeds when glancing at the map I am frequently under-estimating time and distance. In fact I never really got the hang of it: my third day from near Limoges to Burgos seemed to go on for ever (10 hours riding); a great experience but I really was needing to arrive by the end. I pass signs to the 'bath of Brittany' (Bain-de-Bretagne?) and eventually come upon the slip road for Derval half way between Rennes and Nantes (about half an hour after I expected to see it). The typical little French town opened up in front of me, church in the centre, large square and 'yoof' hanging around on scooters and dilapidated mopeds! I stop and read the instructions on finding my friend's house. Go wrong the first time and come upon the first French police I've seen. They watch me go past with a supercilious look; I soon realise I've gone wrong and turn round and head back into town. The police have moved on but as I hunt for the right back lane I see the same police twice more. Each time I feel that their look is a little bit more questioning. A grand arrival at my friends who I haven't seen since I worked in Spain 6 years earlier. We go for supper in the transport cafe 'Le Relais de Derval'. Buffet of salads and various assorted starters and then a main course, wine (or beer) thrown in and bread for a fiver each! Much happy talk and re-acquaintance.

19th Saturday. Derval to Jumilhac-le-Grand. 250 miles.

Fairly early start, still raining! So on with the protective gear. 80 miles later the sun is out and I'm parboiling. Luckily the petrol station at Trellieres where I stop has a loo and I change. My well laid out plan is to go round the Nantes by-pass and pick up the A83 taking me to Niort where I can pick up D roads (like our A's) down toward Limoges. Then turn cross-country at St Junien to get to St Yriex-la-Perche (get your face round that!) and Jumilhac-le-Grand where my next acquaintances (bed) are situated. Somehow I get the wrong exit road (not for the last time) and find myself 'pottering to Poitiers'. By the time I've twigged this I'm near 'Brassiere' (Bressuire) and there is not much point in back-tracking. So in the spirit of adventure I look for a new route! Parthenay, Poitiers, N10 to Angouleme and cut across to Confolens as per plan! As I wind through the a rolling country of stubble fields broken up with nice copses I have the thrill of seeing several Hen Harriers. Near St Junien I turn onto smaller roads that are pretty bumpy. I slow down a little but the Centauro's excellent suspension never feels compromised and my backside is still fine! Turning a corner out of a small village I come upon a bridge over a wide and impressive river; La Vienne says the sign close to which a character is sitting lonely on his scooter, gazing at nothing. I stop to take pictures (not of him), he doesn't move. I leave giving him a nod to which I get no reply. Now I get more curves as we rise through much more wooded areas to Jumilhac.

20th Sunday. Jumilhac-le-Grand to Burgos. 420 miles.

20th Sunday. Jumilhac-le-Grand to Burgos. 420 miles.

On this trip I had many wonderful smell zones. Leaving early in the morning in the middle of France - that wonderful smell of dew wet barley stubble; taking me back to 5.30 am cycling to summer work on the farm as a teenager. Chestnut woods. Bread. Muck spreader. Cut verge grass! And in the middle of this day the hot resinous pine forests of the Lande. I went wrong arriving at Perigueux and ended up following 'Espagne' signs via Toulouse! Realised after a bit that Toulouse was the wrong end of the Pyrenees and so took back roads (curvy at least) to Bergerac. Down through the forests of the Lande. Marmande and Mont-de-Marsan to Orthez. Then St Jean-Pied-de-Port, heading for 'Pampelune'! Bored-looking cops on the roundabout the only indication of the French side of the border. Griffon Vultures. Pulling up the Pyrenees, switch back on switch back. The car in front is right up the boot of the next, he even hoots from time to time. What an idiot. Can't he sense and enjoy the rhythm of the climb, the swing and swing, to and fro, rock faces to one side and trees or huge vistas on the other. Eventually the first car pulls over and the idiot is away. As I go past I make a point of waving and calling 'merci' (French number plates). I hope the driver heard me. For a short while I keep my headlight in 'idiots' rear view mirror to see if he likes being pushed, but what's the point in ruining my 'bien viaje'. I drop back and enjoy the swings of the road showing the near vertical corduroy green mountainsides clothed in oak and beech. Trees blotting the view then glimpses of vertical forest and the expanses of France stretching away behind. At last I reach the high pass of Puerto de Ibaneta, I phone my father and describe the scene, knowing he would have loved to be with me.

I AM NOW 'EN ESPAÑA'! Roncesvalles. Lots of Spanish Guardia at this first village - roadblocks but I am waved through. Pamplona and on for Vitoria (phoned to confirm arrival) and Burgos at last and the excellent Almirante Bonifaz Hotel; bookable over the Internet and with a steel-doored garage to keep the bike safe. I had a salutary experience on this day. When I stopped for petrol I discovered that I had not been careful enough in rigging the panniers and one had worked its way down onto the exhaust (it is necessary to have wedge shaped sports ones anyway because of the swept up pipes). Luckily the heat resistant properties of the Oxford Sports panniers I use prevented a conflagration but I had charred to extinction two 'T' shirts on the inside! Paseo smells, food, Cathedral. I check that the shop is still there for the rosary. Paseo under the plane trees so dark. Sun still bright on the buildings across the river. Everybody is out parading their children, their latest handbag and get up. So smart. Still they dress the little girls up with bows in their hair. The older ladies all with their gold. You meet old friends and acquaintances all the time and pass the words of the day. This is how you build community and society. All ages and experience mix in the paseo. The little children learn the parade and the polite exchanges of news and well wishes. You see the teenagers, some groups all boys or all girls out parading together, they pass and eyes meet and then they wander on to discuss with their friends so and so and so and so. Here a boy rushes with an ice-cream he has just bought, he is trying to catch his 'novia' for whom he has bought it. Concourse, conversation. This is not the land of the skin-tight stretch pants and spilt-gut saggy 'T' shirts. Even those with a bit of 'extra' have style and have made an effort for the paseo. In the Plaza Mayor a silent demonstration: a banner with two white hands. People gather in a big half circle facing the Town Hall with its huge flags drifting in

the slight breeze. Quiet, totally silent this area, further out across the plaza still children run, and chase the pigeons, screaming and laughing; nearby they are quietly hushed. An old man has two pretty little girls in the same green dresses with bows in their hair, one within the circle of each arm. Each holds a piece of cardboard cut from a box with the letters 'ETANO' on it. It takes a minute to realise it says "E.T.A. NO". He holds the girls in front of him, a hand cradled round each brown face as they stand silently facing the Town Hall. There are three and then more TV cameras and newspaper photographers who film the silent, standing crowd that grows as passers-by who come to see what is happening join in. Two policeman watch from the outer edges of the crowd. You can sense that though the crowd is silent it could be aroused, that there is a deep anger against ETA. Now the street lights (about 10' high only, just under the plane tree boughs) have come on. The ceiling of twisted knobbly boughs supporting the thick green canopy that creates cool in the heat of day and darkness and early dusk in the evening before the lights come on. Those seated call out to a passer-by who of course comes over to hear what's new since last Sunday's Paseo. More chairs are pulled up to the table, another order to the waiter. A table starts set out with four chairs and grows to accommodate eight.

21st Monday. Burgos.

Cathedral -chapel of the Constables of Castile. Burgos Castle - Flycatchers, Hoopoe, White Stork on a high gate. Sun has come out and burnt off the early mists and cloud. Buying gifts; Burgos jug, ROSARIES, pottery donkey, flag, knife, Burgos mug, fans. The hot smell of pines after an excellent lunch of tortilla, slice of bread and cerveza. I take siesta on the hot dry grass of the castle mound. More Hoopoes. This day my Spanish has increased four fold; it seems that just the hearing of it re-builds my vocabulary and understanding. I wish I had more days here.

22nd Tuesday. Burgos to Jumilhac-le-Grand. 404 miles.

The long blast to the boarder at San Sebastian. Sun in Burgos but mists and then fogs from Vitoria on to San Sebastian's big roadworks. Lots of police at the border. Many cars are being searched after another ETA attack. Hour after hour of hot strong wind as the miles flow back at 90 to the ton up the Autoroute then motorway through endless forests to Bordeaux. At a services I meet three jolly Bristol bikers on their way to Perigueux. The silhouettes of the dead; all along the roads you pass silent black cut-out shapes, sometimes just the outline of a single man or woman, occasionally there are smaller silhouettes beside them. What must it be like if it was a member of your family that died on that stretch of road? Effective at making one think about safe speeds. On through twisty wooded valleys to Jumilhac's grand castle. Well worth a visit and I believe it is the largest remaining Crusader Castle outside the Holy Land, or some such.

23rd Wednesday. Jumilhac-le-Grand to Derval via Nouic. 270 miles.

Big breakfast after a walk out in the woods. Red squirrels, Buzzard, Golden Oriole (heard). Late start. Warmed up again plenty. Harriers over the fields. Detour to Joe and 'Cako', old friends of my parents, smiling, white haired and so jolly and full of ease. Bees dropping off me in the hall from a swarm I rode through. Back again to the Relais de Derval.

24ᵗʰ Thursday. Derval to Selborne. Aprox 200 miles on land

7.00 wake up and leave by half past. Wide red sky. Smells of dew on new stubble fields. Déforme, Déviation and Prudence, these three French beauties seem to be frequently signposted.
Mistier and colder as I got closer to Cherbourg. Sun came out a bit as we left France behind. Gannets from the ship.

25ᵗʰ Friday Selborne to Aberystwyth. 230 miles.

Rained 50 miles from Aberystwyth... Welcome home to Wales.

Total mileage over 2,100 miles.
Average mpg was 42. Fuel Cost:- aprox £175.00
Oil used - minimal to zero. Back tyre well squared off.

Burgos... again.

Aberystwyth 18th August 2001.

This day I start a quest. A quest that I feel will lead through pain as well as many miles. I ride my steed 'Veloz' to the mountains and plains of northern Spain. I go to tilt and challenge the windmills of loss and grief and confront a life changed. I have a dread as I set out, I continue, as I have for many months to shut off my thoughts from my Father's death. Putting off starting the process of acknowledgement that I know I must go through and that is very largely a reason for this trip. I am off again to Burgos. This time instead of going to Cherbourg and riding down through France having only one full day there I have decided to go by ferry to Bilbao. Less riding time and miles but this way I will get more or less three days in Burgos. Plymouth-Santander is around 24 hrs whereas Portsmouth-Bilbao is 36 hrs, if you are short on time this could be consideration. There are however other plusses to the P&O route (Whales, of which more later)!

Onboard the P&O ferry 'Pride of Bilbao'. August 18th, 19th and 20th.

Here alone in my cabin on the way to Spain I have time to try and search out the truth of his going. Yesterday as we left Portsmouth harbour I was remembering 7 years or so back when Dad came with me to do a renovation job near Alicante. It was a great trip. One full of much friendship and joy. I was very lucky in the relationship I had with my father. We went through a few re-definitions over the years of course, but one of the great things about him was his constant search for new insights and views of the world. He was capable of taking on change. After I had done my degree he made the shift that led from father-son to son-father, to an ever onward expansion and growth of our friendship. He would seek, and take my advice and in many new ways (as he had always done) show me new things and tell me of his latest quest. For he was ever a searcher for truth. The truth that one can never wholly know, the truth of life and light. His paintings and his writings are so often an expression of a chained truth. The truth you cannot hold down though is there in the canvas but chained by his unique experiences of life. Leaving Plymouth that time years ago he told me something of his war time. He had never spoken of it before, but passing Drake Island where he had at one time been stationed brought it back to him. I had so few glimpses into his pre-marriage life and can only get them now at third hand. I was always going to find the opportunity to try and get so much more from him. In these past few years of his cancer we had talked of trying to get together to Spain again. It was not to be, though I so wish it had been. This trip is a pilgrimage; with his spirit and to his memory. There was always so much love in him and though the cancer years were not easy and he was often depressed by It, he could still find that warmth and a big hug that was so much a part of knowing him.

That last night of his life I had left with him a little plastic bull from a bottle of 'Sangre de Toro' wine, telling him that through it we would ride together the roads of Spain. The next morning I held his hand as the grey-sweat of death sheened his face and as he went from us. Now that little bull rides haltered to the key ring on the bike. I sit in the windowless space of this cabin, I guess it has a definite comparison to a hermitage cell; a place for the spiritual and the meditational. A peace comes to me as I write, an understanding, a recognition and a feeling that reminds me of that sense of joy that I felt when he left. I realise that Dad is with me still and will always be. He is along, as we had wanted, on this journey to the Spain of our imaginations. I guess the only way to truly know that he is with me on this trip is to experience it as he would have, to see it as he would have, and to try and garner what he would have. This should

not be too difficult as so much of what I am is down to him. Maybe not in a direct way but in the directions I have developed; sometimes by reacting against, sometimes as a 'result of' his ideas of life and living.

20th - Bilbao to Burgos.

On the Ferry I had eaten a baked 'thing' from one of those 'nancy' display ovens and by this morning as we disembarked was feeling rather green and sick; so the blast out of the dirty, concrete and ugly environs of Bilbao's ferry port was not happy. After I had turned off the motorway and started my cross-country route to Burgos I started to feel better. The start of the ride helped to define the edges; to mark round the experience with darkness, so the rest could shine out the more. At Bilbao you disgorge through warehouses onto a Motorway that carries you off in a rush of traffic. I carefully make my way through the chaos of huge trucks, railway lines and vague road ways onto the motorway which is probably the E70, I am heading for Bilbao and Vitoria (airport) and away from Santander. After a while the motorway divides and I stick to the A68 Vitoria road; more or less the next slip road says Balmaseda. This is the BL 636 and we run in the valley of the Rio Caduaga. At first the road is still pretty big but it gradually gets more interesting and by the time you pass Balmaseda sticking to the BL636 (sometimes now called C6318) for Bercedo it is getting nice. Just after Bercedo one picks up the road to Villarcayo probably called C629. About 7 Km after Villarcayo pick up the N232 southward for a short distance and then turn off on the BU629 for Burgos, this takes you up a great little switchback to the Puerto de la Mazorra (1000m). It is worth turning off to the right just over the crest of the pass and going up to the 'mirador' or look out spot. Here is a great view back the way you have come through the Cantabrian range and in front and to the right of the Val de Valdevielso in which runs the Rio Ebro. Back on the road to Burgos there are some long straights as you travel the higher ground before joining the N623 to drop down the last few miles into Burgos. As it was still early I took to the back roads and ended up at a typical 'end of road' village which I think was Marmellar de Arriba; here there was a big stone trough for clothes washing. Entering Burgos you come in round the north -west end of the castle hill. Took a little bit to work out where I was and a bit more 'round-and-abouting' to find the Hotel (it wasn't quite as close as claimed to the old town and cathedral, in fact across the river).

Have you ever immersed yourself in the outer world alone? Here I am riding; 'El Caballero' the long swells of an arrow straight road through a great sea of stubble fields, gold in the harsh, hot sun. Above, a vast blue sky and a wind like a hair dryer in the face. Hand on left hip I slouch in my saddle, feet loose in the stirrups as my right hand feeds the reigns of speed. Sometimes 70 mph to feel the wind or swoop some gentle bend, at others only 40 or less to soak in some textural view of distant blue and hazy mountains. Espana, I swim in you, smell the dry wheat stubble and sometimes the hot flurry of red, dry dust. I pull in the reins and turn off the engine to sit still and hear the quiet song of the plains and watch high above a drifting Buzzard or the huge 'flying door' of a Griffon Vulture. Have you ridden those mountain passes and pine valleys where you are washed in the scent of pines, cleansed of self? Many native cultures use the smoke of scented wood to cleanse the body and soul. On a bike you don't need to burn the wood just burn the road and wash self. Now here I ride in a miasma of herbal fragrance; almost unbelievably rich, rosemary and marjoram, perhaps thyme and later I see some lavender fields. What a heady cocktail when infused with the suns strength into the hot wind. Only alone do I believe you can truly feel and know such things. Of course there are many moments and sights when one would dearly like to turn to one's 'soul companion' and share, but that is another journey and another experience of life. As the miles pass the outer layers of self become thinner, worn away by the wind and dust and sunflower fields of Spain. Now I am closer and closer to this landscape and can feel myself becoming more and more at one with it.

21st - *Excursion to the Northward.*

I start by heading back out on the N623 towards Santander but turn off left at Quintanaortuno to Mansilla then North up the valley of the Rio Urbel to Huermeces. I wanted to see this place because there were three interesting properties for sale pretty cheap. It is a quite open country with golden stubble fields and a willow and poplar-shaded river. On this road I have my biggest excitement when seeing a bird on a fence post beside the road. I glance quickly at it as I pass by at probably 40mph. Its unusual colouring and form imprint an almost photographic image on my mind's eye and I cannot immediately place this bird of prey. Looking in my bird book later I immediately recognise a Red-Footed Falcon that shouldn't really have been there! I ended up on the N627 and again head North toward Santander for a short way before turning right onto the BU601 toward Masa. I cross N623 and enter some pinewood plantations that smell great, I am now on the BU503. I cross BU629 (P de la Mazorra-Burgos road) and am now on the BU502 to Poza de la Sal. It is well worth a detour; a great valley view and a ruined castle that I unfortunately did not have

time to explore. Down to Cornudilla where I turn north on N232 (Santander) just as far as Cerecada and here go right up through lovely forest and round a long lake. On up the Val de Valdevielso through its dusty villages, with the hard ridged mountains scoring upward to the right, the lush Ebro valley bottom to the left. At the end of the valley one rejoins the route of yesterday just below the P de la Mazorra and so take the BU629 back to Burgos.

22nd - *Excursion to the Southward.*

Riding slow now through a small village off the beaten track, the houses all growing up dusty out of the roadway it seems. On a seat outside their door old folks stare as I go by. Sometimes I nod or salute and sometimes I get a smile or a reply that crosses the divides of our existence. If I stop in a village that feels friendly my 'poco Espagnol' will often draw a friendly "Hola, Buenos dias".

After a few days of hearing only Spanish, of attempting to speak only Spanish (so for long periods I speak not all), as I ride I begin to talk to myself in my rudimentary Spanish. Spanish that has drifted into me with the sights and sounds of this vast and enthralling country. How little do I need the constant chatter of my normal life; now I only speak when it is really needful; "Uno Cafe solo, por favor"! I have space in my head that is empty, not of all thought, but enough to be able to draw in the world and to see things more clearly.

In a little village I leave the through road, ride into the narrow double-donkey-wide lanes and find a bar next to a big stone water trough. Fresh clean water runs spouting out of a pipe and all the village dogs and children seem to come to drink. One little boy peddles up on his plastic 'Police car'. I sit outside the cool dark bar and soak up some more hot sun as the bike, almost dipping its head to drink at the trough 'tinks' and 'tonks' as the hot engine cools. My simple requests have produced half a large flat loaf bread filled with thinly sliced ham and saucer of olives, with a 'pequeño' glass of Cerveza, agua and a cafe solo to follow. I have lunched so richly that it is an effort to say goodbye to my new-found best friend with the doleful brown eyes, long rabbit-ears and ever ready black nose; in these villages you can find the most amazing collection of motley dogs. Sometimes it appears a mad cartoonist has been around mixing up the head off one breed with the body of another and the tail from yet another. I say my "adios" to the senora of the bar and receive my "bien viaje" to bless my onward journey. Sometimes this caballero reaches a stretch of road which lifts and winds through more rolling and partially wooded country; my steed champs at the bit and I give him his head as we challenge the road ahead. We must concentrate fully on that stretching strip of (mostly) tarmac. Here a pothole, and look that next bend the surface has been massaged when 'beating' hot by some big truck. A great ruck-groove around the outside of the curve, if we can get it right we can use the inside of the ruck to make up for the lack of camber and whip us round in a gloriously pleasurable swoop. Sometimes though we see the need for caution as the ruck looks more like a cross-grained plough furrow. Good old 'Veloz' barely shakes his head and jumps the ridge and then picks up his hooves to leap forward down the straight to the next sweep and swoop. The new windmills of La Mancha are towering high-tech wind farms sweeping their arms with awesome sense of ponderous work. I tilt only at the windmills of my mind. I find some of that peace and acceptance of my father's death that I have been searching for. Here I feel his artist's eye with me, seeing and painting for me the far reaching textures of the plains. He is with me because of his own paintings of Spain. I seem to see now in paint; the *gold ochre* fields that patchwork with the *burnt umber* and *dusty rose* of ploughed fields. Edged hard here and there by stark grey rock formations. Deep green of pines that wash and break against the hard yellow crags of the Ebro valley. These cliffs painted with water-colours of pale yellows and pinks and here and there a run of black ink has leaked and wept down from the hard edge against the sky. To my left mostly hidden by the flickering green hands of the 'Choppo' poplars is the river. Like me it sometimes rushes on headlong towards another dip and bend, and at others seems content to meander slowly and grow a

few water lilies and collect ducks. The old men who watch my slow trot through their village or past their small field of maize seem stamped from almost all the same mould... Faded blue of often washed work clothes, short and square with long years of work under this hot sun, and yet you sense a vitality. The long years have soaked in the sun's strength and they use it sparingly. The woman who beats her mats at the doorway; proclaiming her part and her housework (but also checking up on the passer by), is now in a flowery print dress. In the old days and further south one saw many more wearing black. All black for their perhaps long gone husband. The old ways in which a young man must work hard and into his thirties before he had the price, or was likely through death to inherit a house with which to wed led, and still perhaps does lead in some areas, to very early-widowed women. Of course in the past they could never re-marry but must busy there lives with their children and grandchildren's doings.

I ride out to a large reservoir (Embalse). Stopping to look over the view I hear the music of big melodious cowbells from across the valley. Three Bonelli's eagles soar overhead and three Great Crested Grebes swim serenely on the deep blue water. Cicadas chirr, and the tick-tick of the (slightly) cooling engine punctuates the twittering of massed Swallows, Martins and Swifts and the gentle lapping of the waters edge. There are such wonderful smells on this trip; of rosemary and oregano and pine woods particularly in the Sierra de la Demanda, Arlanzon valley and Sierra de Niela. Sometimes I ride past fields of Sunflowers hiding their faces from the sun, dropped heads with bright yellow hair falling around to shade their eyes. I started off on the N120 for Logrono but not far out of Burgos turn right to Arlanzon.

At Arlanzon turn left onto the BU-P8201 to the Embalsa de Uzquiza. Follow round the Embalse and on down the Rio Arlanzon on the now BU-P8101 to Pineda. A superb area of lake, oak and pine forests, crags and rocks with many great places to stop and picnic. On to Barbadillo de Herreros and now on the C113 (to Logrono) at the (1240m) pass after Monterrubio de Demanda turn right to Huerta de Arriba. This is where I had my great bar lunch and met the dog. Now towards Niela with a side trip up towards Laguna Negra de Niela (2000m). This whole Sierra de Niela is a National Reserve and full of stunning scenery. The black lake of Niela looked well worth a visit and was obviously a popular picnic spot with the Spanish. Now take the BU822 to Quintanar de la Sierra. In this valley I passed a brilliant looking camp site; rushing rocky river, well spaced out plots with barbecue places in amongst pine trees and a big clean looking (from a distance anyway) toilet block. Back towards Burgos on BU-P8221 to Salas de Los Infantes. I didn't try and find the Necropolis marked on the map near Quintanar. After Salas join the N234 (Burgos) to Hortiguela where I turned left on the C110 for Covarrubias. One passes the Ermita de San Pedro de Arlanza which probably was worth stopping to look over, (saw Griffon Vultures very close here). At Covarrubias I went right for Mecerreyes where there were some fascinating houses built right into the hillside. On to Cuevas de San Clemente and left up N234 back to Burgos.

23rd and 24th - return Ferry.

A faster trip back to Bilbao via Briviesca and again up the Val de Valdevielso, Vilacayo etc. One and three quarter to two hours but pushing along fairly, considering the road and the odd patch of mist and fog on the northerly side of the Cantabrians. P&O have an arrangement and commitment to a Cetacean Survey of the Bay of Biscay. In practical terms, if you go up to the Helicopter deck you will find an enthusiastic (twitcher mad) group watching the sea through binoculars and telescopes for the first 'blow' or sign of a whale or dolphin. I found myself getting caught up in the camaraderie of the whale watchers and realising the thrill as a shout of "blow at 10 O'clock" causes a rush across the deck to see the fleeting, leaping shapes of Dolphins or the long-lounging, sleepy Sperm Whale like some huge flotsam beam adrift on the swells. I ended up spending hours up on the deck and by journey's end had seen Sperm, Minke and Pilot Whales, Striped and Common Dolphins and leaping Yellow-Fin Tuna as well as the quick-lighted Shearwaters and Black terns. As we entered the Solent a wonderful surprise was a Melodious Warbler on one of the bridge stays, vying with the attractions of the Festival Of the Sea stately 'tall ships' as we entered Portsmouth.

On the morrow I shall be back home in Wales and will have to catch up with work as well as try to assimilate all the richness and the grieving of my adventure.

Aberystwyth

Concentración Internacional España Moto Guzzi Club 2002 Alcorisa

25th June.

I have finally got the bike packed having decided to leave all the bad weather gear at home and trust to chance and a lighter load. I am wearing my Gialli jeans and jacket, but just in case the weather doesn't behave I have some cheap over-trousers and a waterproof nylon coat. Off Veloz and I go.

First stop is my friendly Kwik-Fit to check my tyre pressures. I swing carefully into the cavernous interior and over to the air hoses. The guys are happy for me to check the pressures and up them a bit for the added weight. The sun continues to shine as I work my way into the new weight of the bike and the fact that I am actually on my way to Spain again. The first 25 miles from Aberystwyth are incredibly familiar but are always great fun; here the swoops and tightening corners, great views and @*^**$ caravans all make the A44 such a gas. At Llangurig I tell myself my safety mantra "half hour is coming up so watch the concentration". I have noticed that though I start off very aware of my riding after half an hour I can get blasé and think I have it all in hand: then you let your mind drift a bit, as one tends to do in the car and suddenly you are going into a corner too fast or didn't see that plank in a 'fiasco' who just pulled out.

It is a great road this, the A470, a nice mix of straights and curves through lovely country. Rhayader to Builth Wells and onward, the thought of a week on my own and going to Spain brightening the scenery that whisks back behind. Now with the rushing river Wye keeping me company till Llyswen where it turns off to visit Hay on Wye. At Talgarth the road does an extreme right-angled (now by-passed) corner tight-bounded by houses that bear the marks left by car transporters and other HGV's who have difficulty getting round. Here there is an excellent tea and second-hand bookshop; for me it is almost impossible not to come out with a book and today I give it a miss. Swinging on up the tight bends that will skirt the high ridges of the Black Mountains. Past Tretower which has a medieval manor house and castle to visit; but not today, now the focus is much farther ahead. Abergavenny with its tea shop by the bus station, during summer colonised by bikers from far and near. I don't stop but swing on; now the B4598, bike and me, swift and smooth, despite the narrow winding roads and odd cars to overtake. After Usk the B4235 brings one on, till suddenly the view opens and the Severn Bridge looms in the distance. Quick now through Chepstow's edge and blast across the bridge. 110 miles or so, probably under 2 hours and time for petrol in the Severn Services of the M4. At the services I have one of those brief exchanges that you have with another biker; he talks of how easy his Deuville is to just get on and go. Certainly with its integral luggage design it looks a good tourer. I even considered one once but decided it would be underpowered and rather bulky for those scratching moments round the hills and sheep of Wales. M4 - M5 southward we go. I have one call that I have decided to make before my sisters. I had not been back since the funeral to the field in which my father was laid to rest more than a year ago. Now I think I can encompass it and turn off the Motorway to smaller roads that take me to the aptly named End O'Lane. Here with a rather heavy heart I park the bike and walk through a farmyard and across one field to another that gently slopes to the North. The grass is un-grazed or cut and knee height. It is like wading through clinging water, or is it my own feelings that drag at each step. But here next to the Wren-singing copse is his place. No marker but I know where I stood on that hardest of days. Looking outward to the Polden Hills and feeling the peace of the place my ache is eased. Dad will be travelling with me to Spain again as he would have so loved to have done.

26th June.

I get up early enough to have a very easy blast down to Plymouth. Arriving with time in hand to chat to other bikers of which there are many. I try to think of useful phrases to talk to a girl with a Suzuki 250 cruiser who is obviously Spanish. She is returning to her home in Murcia after a year in London. Pleasantries are passed as we wait to board. At last the boarding is done; I am glad I brought an extra ratchetable luggage strap to secure the bike, rather than depending on finding enough pieces of greasy rope. This is Brittany Ferries and they haven't been as bike-friendly or helpful as P&O are. Unfortunately the shorter trip to Santander (rather than Portsmouth - Bilbao) is a *must* for my tight schedule. Clearing Drake Island my thoughts return to my father and the time we travelled to Spain together with my van full of doors and a fitted kitchen for the job near Alicante. The sea is flat the whole trip and though I see Gannets, shearwater, and Fulmar there are no whales. Last year on the P&O Bilbao route there were many to be seen, but I guess we are that much further out and off the continental shelf.

27th June.

On deck as we approach Spain we can see great banks of cloud hiding most of the Cantabrian mountains - sunny Spain! In Santander it is raining, downer. First in so last off and we have been advised to go out west then round Santander on the bypass as they are in the process of digging up half the roads in

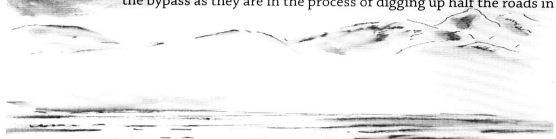

the centre of town on the normal route to the south. I have decided to risk not putting on waterproofs as it is warm (around 30 degrees) despite the light drizzle. Also I have experienced the cloud curtain of these mountains before and expect to clear them at the top of the main pass inland. Anyway I gaily set off as directed but then on a whim turn off with a vague idea of cutting back to the road out that I know, but end up in the upper town. Though somewhat lost this does have the advantage that I find a small supermarket to buy supplies at. Now for the first real attempt to get the old Spanish working; try for directions to Burgos. He understood my request and I understood a fair bit of the answer and find my way okay to the right road, though I do one bit of round-and-round when accidentally getting onto the Bilbao road at the outskirts. Three access roads later and I'm right. Now we start the relatively short, sharp climb up the Cantabrians. A bit of rain but nothing too bad to start with, but it becomes very foggy by the time I approach the Puerto del Escudo (1011 mts) - 20 feet visibility. But within a mile or so as I run down to the Embalse del Ebro the sun is breaking through. As I am hitting 120 miles from my last fill up in Exeter I spot a petrol station with another bike pulled up - in I go. Graham runs a Hotel on the Isle of Arran with his wife normally, but now he is delivering (by riding it naturally) a Harley-D to Valencia. We talk and as he has never ridden in Spain before we ride together as we wend our way to Burgos. I head straight for the Plaza Mayor, where I know we can easily park up and relax into - SPAIN! We sit at one of the Plaza edge cafes and order light refreshments; in my case a café solo (short, black and strong). I have a pequeño paseo (little walk) round the Plaza and through to the riverfront as Graham watches the bikes. In the Plaza kids play football, and one adult briefly joins in; now España is seeping into me. Graham is headed for Soria where he is going to stay the night. I am headed in the same direction for a short while, until I turn off for a campsite that I saw the previous year. I breezily, and with great panache pick up the N120 road; except I get it wrong and head for Leon instead of Logroño. Never mind, the forty mile detour was a nice intro to Spanish back roads; I re-plot our course back through Isar and the valley of the Rio Hormazuela until we are again heading toward Soria.

Now on the N234 the difference in our bikes is becoming more apparent; the Harley is not comfortable anywhere above 60 mph and re-fuelling becomes a worry at 90 miles. Veloz and I are happy at 60-80 and only need to drink at around 140. I choose to continue keeping Graham company for a while longer on the N234 after I would have turned of at Salas de los Infantes. But when we petrol up at San Leonardo de Yague we agree to part ways as I will very soon have to turn northward for the Sierra de la Demanda. I pull up at a roadside bar in Navaleno and wave him onward. I would like something to eat but of course find that I can only get a beer before 9pm. So Veloz and I turn our noses north for Quintanar de la Sierra over a 1351 mts pass (my maths makes it a good 4,000 feet) which is bigger than any peak in my Welsh back yard! Last year when I spent my week (3 nights in Spain) exploring a 100 mile or so radius around Burgos I spotted this great looking campsite with river and trees as I came down from the Sierra de la Demanda. Now, as a fairly long day wanes, I am trying to find it again. I go past the way to it, as I head out of Quintanar, because the access road seems to be through a timber yard. I wind up where I can see it across the river and have to turn round and go back. Finally I find the way in. In Reception I find a very pleasant young Spaniard who responds well to my assumption that he does not speak English and whom I do my best to communicate with in bad (very bad) Spanish. After a while it turns out he has a fair bit of English and apart from welcoming me and taking details etc informs me that there are two other British bikers staying here. Very old bikes he says; my interest is naturally aroused. As I ride onto the site I spot two vintage 1000cc Vincent's and a couple of tents. I pick a spot fairly close and set up my own camp. The theory was to run the bike onto one edge of the tarp, then peg half out as a ground-sheet to one side, and finally to tie the remainder as 'roof' up onto the handlebars and seat. Nice idea. Even seems to work! Having set up camp I go to talk to the Vincent owners - Roy and Wilf. they are 75 and 80! I just hope

I make it as far as they have and looking as spry. Each year they set off together for many weeks touring; somewhere in Europe! They will stay a few days here a few days there, sometimes they told me they only move 20 miles to another campsite; just as they wish. THAT is the way to spend one's retirement! Most of this I find out later when we go to the little Bar/Restaurant that

is integral to the site. We seem to be virtually the only campers so I wonder that the place is open. Of course it is at least half 11 before we leave after drinks and food and much talk. They tell me of the Necropolis in walking distance that is well worth a visit. Deciding to go in the morning they lend me a little map/leaflet about it as well as a small rucksack so I can take my camera etc. When we return to our tents I realise that a 'Katabatic' (I do remember something from 'A' level Geog) wind seems to be flowing down the valley and I begin to think that perhaps I should have positioned everything the other way round. At this point (foolishly) I feel too wined and dined to bother and decide that it won't matter. As the night progresses the wind rises. Rushing hard down the valley from the mountain tops, not only cold but very, very noisy! I can't sleep as it bangs the tarp around my ears. About 1 am I have to do something. I manage to unhitch the tarp from the bike and wrap it tight around me. Now it can't bang! I finally get to sleep then. A long day really.

28th June.

I had not brought a camping stove and was enormously grateful to Wilf for the cup of tea that got me going. Luckily I had brought alternative foot ware so I didn't have to pressure-cook my feet in boots on my excursion to the Necropolis. I follow a logging track through the pine woods, Roy had said that there was a short cut through the woods at a branch of the track. I seemed to

get the start of it but soon lose it. But from the leaflet map I could see that all I needed to do was follow the small stream and I would come out on a track again. After nearly a kilometre's fast walk I was getting well warmed up, and finding a slightly larger pool I decided to cool down. Stripping off I sat in the water; and lost my breath completely

- a quick splash in the freezing water and onward. Finally arriving at the Necrópolis de Cuyacabras. "Gran necrópolis altomedieval del s. XI con 166 tumbas antropomórficas y 13 nichos excavados en la superficie de la roca. Rodeado de una tupida masa y robles le confieren al lugar un aire

mágico." Very much a magic air - a sense of timelessness as following a little footpath I suddenly come out onto this large rock, half hidden amongst the pine and oak trees. The hot sun beats down on the extraordinary body shaped holes carved out of the rock. No funeral charges then, just get put in a hole in the rock until nature has disposed of you and someone else can get in. Having amused myself with the timer on my camera I have to turn round and get a move on. I have quite a few miles to go. Back at the campsite I quickly get packed up before heading to the Bar for lunch with Roy and Wilf. A very nice boccadillo later I bid them farewell. Get the bike and go to Reception to pay. The young man is friendly and his father (who I think is the campsite owner or manager) gets interested when he finds out I am going to Alcorisa. He is a luminary in the local La Jota club. La Jota is a special type of particularly Aragonese singing; they wear chequered bandanas - 'el cachirulo' (mainly on their heads) and special costumes. La Jota has a lot of social importance. Senor Joaquin gives me a copy of the 'Amigos de la Jota' magazine with himself and the main man in Alcorisa ringed with red felt pen, who he wants me to find (in a certain bar). One feels so inadequate when one's language skills are so poor. Anyway we part mucho amigos. I head south-east picking up the N-234 again. 70 Km later I am by-passing Soria and reeling in the 100 odd Km to Calatayud. I love these long roads, great sweeps of land with distant mountains and the feeling of Spain spreading endlessly in front of the

spinning front wheel. Occasionally I stop to take photos or for petrol. After Calatayud comes Darocha and then Caminreal where I turn left onto the N-211 for Alcaniz. The road, that has often been a thread running across a vast patchwork blanket of fields and small villages, gets more twisty, twining through rocky passages and the odd tunnel. Coming round a bend the road becomes a flyover as a gorge opens up beneath it. A great knife-edged slab of rock to one side, water-cut arroyo the other. I pull over and turn off the engine. It ticks its heat away and I feel the silence and still warmth as I get out my camera. I finally arrive at Alcorisa just after 7pm. After a little asking I get to the Municipal Hostel, a large modern building across the river from the main town centre. Now I finally meet Carlos 'Gutenberg'. I had wondered whether he spoke

any English as we had started our contact when he asked if he could publish my first Burgos trip account having come across my website. Normally I practised my Spanish in e-mailing him although sometimes including English, I somehow thought he must know some - he didn't, and neither did his wife Gloria or son. I also find out later why the confusing German name - it is his nickname because he was or is a typesetter. Anyway despite his very rapid Spanish I manage to get the drift. Over this weekend I saw why he is such an esteemed Guzzista. Like an amiable bear he greets everyone with such warmth and good humour. It is evident that he and his family put enormous energy and hours into the club. I inspect the sleeping arrangements, dormitories of bunk beds each having its own shower and toilet; all very clean. I grab a bunk and get cleaned up. I come down to the front to find other Guzzis steadily arriving. By about nine when I get a lift in Carlos's car to a bar my stomach is feeling pretty empty. Unfortunately there is not much relief as this is a nuts, crisps and beer event. It is good fun though as others arrive on foot and on bikes; each new arrival means the re-positioning of yet more tables to accommodate us all -we end up taking over the whole stretch of 'road' that the bar claims. I try very hard to a) follow conversation, and b) occasionally reply, but only two days into Spain my language centre is still very slow. It is a great relief when finally sometime after ten we head back to the Hostel. Now three long tables are set out for the 80'ish present. A 3

course meal with wine included follows. So much Spanish I frustratingly cannot understand but very nice people who try and include me. At 12.15 am I finally quit as a large number head out to the bars again. I may have only ridden 668 miles (nearly 1400 miles from home) in three days to get here but it has been tiring and my body clock has not adjusted to Spanish 'time'. Some of the other occupants of my room return around 2 and then some more at 3, and at 4! To make things worse there is one guy whose snoring is most reminiscent of a bag of piglets fighting in a sack! Not a brilliant night's sleep for an old wus like me.

29th June.

I get up at 9 and find some black-mud coffee and rusks with jam for breakfast. I have found it rare to get what one would call a decent breakfast in any Hotel or Hostel in Spain; they seem to figure you either don't really need it or you'll head to a cafe where you can get decent coffee and croissant or other bread or pastries. There is not a rush for breakfast but things slowly get going. After a bit Carlos and Gloria and their son set up a table and the stuff to register everybody. 51 Euros (40€ for Sat-Sun) for two big meals (wine inc) per day and 'rusks' and coffee for breakfast, if you got up in time. A bandanna (el cachirulo), club mag, cap, wallet, pen, and lighter were also included. I also buy the T-shirt for 9€. A note:- when filling in the registration form for distance to get there put down total travelled, not as I did just my riding - some Germans beat me to one of the awards as they counted train distance from Germany to Marseille! More bikes arrive. Around midday we again go to the bar, this time on bikes - even more arranging of tables. About 1.30 I go to get petrol and then back to the Hostel from where I watch a fairly spectacular thunderstorm roll up. Sometime after 2 we sit down again to eat. I have now come across a very pleasant couple from Madrid who deal in antiques who have some English, and a German Robert whose English is very good. It is actually quite a relief to have a conversation without so much brain effort. Lunch is finished some time after 4. I decide a forty wink siesta might be in order but have hardly lain down when I hear 'vamos'! The road has dried and we are going on parade. Off we all go with much hooting of horns and general fandango. We go round the town, diving down some ridiculously narrow alleyways between tall overhanging houses. There is a central gutter with sloping cobbled sides and some very tight corners, lots of fun! We end up at the Town Sports Centre were we get the Civic treatment (speeches) and one free drink. People are drifting around and drinking but I need to wake up so I go for a blast toward Alcaniz. A beautiful long straight road with bare fields to either side and no traffic. I can't resist and wind Veloz up to 200kph. Back in Alcorisa well woken I go back to the bar, park up and get

myself an orange juice. Soon I meet an interesting Frenchman with a Cali. He is an engineer and lives in Barcelona. He is staying in a Hotel just along the main street from where we are which has a safe place for his bike. So one doesn't have to mess in at the Hostel if you don't want to. Robert joins us and the talk flows. Around 10pm we sit down for the main banquet which includes the awarding of trophies for this that and the other - amid many jokes and ribaldry. I get one for distance but Robert is cheesed that I didn't get the first one which went to some other Germans who he said had taken the train to Marseille. Anyway I got a Maico model Centauro, which I prefer to their small tinny cups! The meal finishes about 1 am - of course everybody heads off to the bars.

30th June.

Rusk and coffee at 10. Then I started putting my stuff together. Discover however that we are all going on a ride out. A Guardia Civil car turns up and after various discussions about which I have absolutely no idea we set off led by the flashing lights. Again we go through the two-donkey streets with its cobbles and nice slippery tiled gutter in the middle. Much booming of Guzzi exhausts as we go up these narrow streets on a Sunday morning. Surprisingly the locals don't seem to mind. Then we go out of town and miles up into the hills to a tight little village square which has difficulty with twenty to thirty bikes and the cop car. For a while even the cop does not know which of the 4 exits to take. Eventually a decision is made and of we go again. Up and up to a big Embalse and beyond, great rocky hillsides and lots of 'fear defeators': ('quita miedo' - gets rid of fear!) big white-painted concrete blocks at the roads edge where there is a drop. Huge Griffon Vultures fly very close alongside giving one the eye, perhaps hoping the defenders won't work. A long switch-back pull that seriously discommodes some bikes as we are running at 30-40 mph and around the dreaded 3-4,000 rpm stutter point for many older Guzzis. Eventually we come to the end of tarmac and the road continues as loose gravel! Oops! Cop and all, we turn around and head back down. Somehow this time we miss the tiny square, and get to Alcorisa via another round of the very narrow streets (it now occurs to me that perhaps this was solely for our benefit so we could hear our own exhausts nicely). Back to a nice lunch of various meat slices, olives, wine and bread. Most reckon the free wine is a bit rough and needs water or Casera (very sweet Spanish lemonade) to make it drinkable; of course as an English pleb I quite like its roughness, but alternate wine and water in the interests of safety. A final round of photos and 'hasta luego y adios' and everyone heads off in their different directions.

A few kilometres later I stop for petrol just as rain starts. Also at the pumps I meet up with a group from Zaragoza, a little more sputtering conversation and onward. I decide to make for Burgos and a Hotel as the weather is worsening with much wind and thunder and lightning. I try racing the rain trying to stay ahead of the front but after 200 miles I stop to re-tog up with waterproofs at a roadside Hostel with a big roof as it has caught, and overtaken me! Here I meet some English bikers on Harley-Davidsons, a couple of which are pink! They are quitting and booking in here after coming up from Valencia and two weeks of very hot sun, lucky bastards. I travel on, eventually arriving at the Felice Gonzales Hotel; phew, they have a room. I dive straight into a hot bath and then somewhat recovered, phone home. Later I go into town for the paseo. Everything is very lively with street theatre and TV cameras by the municipal theatre. After some rather expensive tapas I get caught up with a kind of 'battle of marching bands', or maybe its just a great procession and fiesta. The bands play jazz or marches and are all very well turned out and drilled. When they stop in the Plaza Mayor there is more great jazz. Eventually after dark the day has got to me and I return to the hotel. I was going to come out again but then suddenly felt very tired so stayed in and watched an amazing fireworks display over the city. Huge bursts of many coloured flowers and whistling, shrieking, coloured rain. Huge bangs (that shook the window of my room) and star bursts that looked to cover the whole city. I watched and listened to some of it through the window but also on the television which gave me panoramic views from many viewpoints, I must remember this fiesta and try to catch it again

31st June.

Got up late really, 8.30ish to 9. Went straight out for breakfast as I remembered the hotel's 'desayuno' coffee as terrible. Bar Garbo under the plane trees for cafe solo and croissant. A hot and much better day. Walked way up the Avenue Vitoria and round about looking for shops and banks; eventually started trying to get cash with my visa card and ran into a brick wall. The problem was I didn't have my PIN number; I had figured to be able to sign instead. Nada! Gave up in the end and had to eat posher (mas caro) where I can pay by signing a visa slip. I am eking out my last 20 euros on small stuff. A nice lunch by the cathedral (they took visa); Castilian soup with chorizo in it, half a small chicken and chips with some salad, little jug of vino tinto, water, naranja and cafe solo. Then up to the castle to look for Hoopoes; found only some feathers, very sad. But there were Crossbill and Black Redstart, many Serin and Goldfinch all of which made up for the lack of Hoopoes. Back to the hotel about 4pm for a late siesta. Some time after 5 got up and took the bike out to get petrol. I ended up going out on the old Bilbao road from last year just for a bit of a blast. Rocky outcrops, fields of many patchwork colours, pine smells; filled up on the way back. Out then to get some supplies for the boat on visa; had tried going to Lidl, but of course, cash only! So rather posh grub! Had to repack a bit to get it all in. Now 8.45 and one beer down, trying to last till it is late enough to get a meal in the little square by the Palace of the Constables of Castilla. In England we sit down to eat and perhaps talk a little between courses, in Spain you sit down to talk with a bit of food here and there so it takes a long time. On my own I have just about managed to make the first two courses take half an hour. The typical Spanish meal seems to take at least two hours; at a bare minimum! Walking the streets I pass a dog food shop, in the doorway is a beautiful little pup, sort of Alsatian, but not, brown and black with slightly floppy ears. He looked at me with a very wistful air! I had to stop and go back for a second look, he gave me the eye again. Good thing I couldn't have taken him on the bike!

1st July.

Up at 6.30, left hotel at about 7.15. Very foggy on the top of the Cantabrians but arrived in time for coffee, croissant and petrol before going for the boat. Rough at sea though the next day better; we come into Plymouth an hour late.

2nd July.

Just before Abergavenny on the way home, the oil light starts flashing. Oh Sheeeeet! Stop and find oil on my boot, the hose to the cooler behind the front wheel has sprung a leak! A.A. Relay home. DOH!!!!!

Burro at Santa Casilda.

El Escorial

Researching Arizona.

(Spain in October 2003)

For six months the plan had been a fortnight. Two weeks to find a desert. Two weeks biking in Spain! So far my annual trips to Spain on my Centauro 'Veloz' have always taken place within the framework of one week. Two was going to be so relaxed... Except for the fact that I had to find a desert. You see the 'reason' for this year's trip was RESEARCH; cast-iron, eh! It goes like this; down near Almeria in southern Spain is where Serge Leone filmed spaghetti westerns like 'The Good, The Bad and the Ugly'. These are set in Arizona. I have written a novel set in 1870's Arizona. Ése es el (That's it)! In order to finish off my novel I need to get the feel of the desert, the smell and taste of dust and hot rock, the prick of cactus... So for months I work out different itineraries that take me there. It being two years since I had been down through France I rather fancied the long route, but on the other hand, how about circumnavigating Spain; down one side and back up the other. I could take in Burgos, Alicante, Almeria, Granada, Sevilla, Salamanca, Leon - an adventure in one paragraph. 3,000 miles or more, what an exciting and enticing prospect. As an extremely busy year sped by and time became compressed, the dates for this trip kept getting put back and compromised; at one point it seemed I would not get any trip at all. Finally with great difficulty a one week slot at the beginning of October was found. Frantic arithmetic and Ferry timetables followed as I tried to make Almeria. I couldn't make it work, not within anything like legal road speeds. So were there any other deserts in Spain? Internet searches, bookshop porings and riflings, map and atlas study produced two other instances of 'desierto' on the maps of Spain. One near Valencia - Desierto las Palmas and the other the Desierto de Calanda, north of Teruel. The former was a bit far but the latter had potential, it was very close to Alcorisa where I had been the previous year for the Moto Guzzi Club of Spain Rally, so I knew it was not difficult to do in the week, and I knew the way. Plans began to coalesce. The ferry timetables and prices set against my dates meant that I had to go down to Bilbao from Portsmouth and come back through France to Cherbourg - Portsmouth. With two weeks to go the Ferry was booked! Then problems with my side-stand returned. The previous year I had only just got it fixed in time to go. Panic time! I decided to weld up a bracket to clamp the side stand bracket, crude but effective! I am booked on the nine o'clock sailing from Portsmouth to Bilbao, Saturday 29th September. The last two days at home are fraught with hurried preparation and attempts to avoid and cover for crises; normally either the computers or the central heating breaks down as soon as I leave. I have decided to try and camp in Spain and stay with friends on the run back up through France. The bike is rather loaded and as our weather is not very clement a lot of extra insulation and weather protection is required. I finally set off at 2pm. The early miles as always were mixed euphoria and worry. What have I forgotten, why am I doing this? Then: YYYYESSS! I'm on my way to Spain! Just my horse and me. As the miles click round and we start to get into the groove all the negatives begin to be lost in our wake. Skimming along the A470 with the River Wye tumbling and thrashing its way beside the road, the euphoria wins out. This is the way to travel; anticipate the overtaking and be ready to use the great torque of the Centauro engine. These winding 'A' roads through great Welsh scenery are made for a bike with the ability to keep average speeds in the 65 - 80 mph range, without changing gear. Roll on at 4-5,000 rpm in fourth and you shove past the tin buffaloes, roll back and Guzzi engine/shaft braking pulls you in behind the next beast. Here is the smooth - no braking (unless really necessary); road-reading at that level where you are one with machine, constantly assessing and re-assessing, unaware of anything but the backward flow of cars and lorries, the forward flow of

bends and straights and the next, soon to be victim, of a well executed slap-past. The Severn Bridge is just over 110 miles of twisting roads, tight villages, and the small Welsh towns of Rhayader, Builth Wells and Abergavenny. I think my best time is 1 and 3/4 hours; I have to say that I rarely go over eighty. M4 to Newbury, pass the long-gone caravan site at the gates of Greenham Common - now an Industrial Estate, skim the never-never land of Basingstoke. Alton and now Selborne where I stop for a break with my welcoming favourite Aunt. An hour later and egg and beans heavier I am back on the road to Portsmouth. The first dramas of the trip unfold at the check in; a biker with a dislocated shoulder and serious pain is vainly trying to pursue his vanishing holiday as the ship's doctor is called to have a look at him. The confusions and delays at the kiosk cause some of the Mercedes and Rovers to wind down their windows and talk to a motorcyclist! Of course that weird camaraderie of 'the boat trip' soon kicks in as those on their way to their villa on the Costa chat to the lower classes. Eventually we are on-board and strapping down the bike. The old pillows are well worth grabbing, I use them stuffed into the gap between bike and railing to try and ensure that the bike can't move; always leave it in gear as well. I haven't yet suffered damage but have seen a few broken indicators, though in at least one case this was probably due to the later-arriving car travellers trying to get past with their suitcases. The first step into the cabin is always a bit bizarre. Over the year one seems to have forgotten how enclosed this little white room is; stand anywhere and touch two walls! The ferry timetable with its 'luxury cruise' look seems to beguile one into a vague expectation of a port-holed cabin with space to dance. Of course if you pay enough you can have that. Anyway it doesn't take that long to get settled in and comfortable with one's little box. If finances are a little stretched it is well worth bringing as much food for the journey as you can. It is easy to spend three days worth in Spain in one meal on board. Having said that, I didn't bring much more than bread, and despite better intentions end up having a slap-up meal and shutting my eyes to the price I pay for a bottle of Rioja. Plymouth-Santander is quicker, but more expensive, and you don't get to see any whales. This trip there are not many, but a great view of hundreds of dolphins creaming their way towards us and at the last moment diving under the boat. The water so clear that one can see the power of their tail strokes as they accelerate for each leap from the water.

5 am day 2.

I can't get back to sleep and head for the deck. There is hardly anyone about. As I climb the gangways I breathe deep trying to smell Spain on the gusting wind. For some reason I half expected dawn to be breaking, though there is a hint of light on the horizon to the east. Later I realise this must have been the lights of San Sebastian and Biarritz as the first Spanish dawn does not arrive for many hours; bringing with it a damp grey drizzle. As we ride off the boat I comfort myself with the thought that I will probably get clear of it as I climb over the Cantabrians. As always, I am heading first for Burgos (for lunch) before heading further East to the campsite at Quintanar de la Sierra. On the quayside I pick a car that looks like it knows its way out and follow it through the maze of warehouses, trucks, fork-lifts, rail tracks, and out finally to the spaghetti junction of the coast motorway: Full of thundering lorries and speeding cars, it is a bewildering start. I take care on the slip roads getting into the traffic watching out for the inside lane turning into slip road. Having done this before I am not unduly worried and soon pick up the BL636 through Balmaseda, Villarcayo and via the Puerto de la Mazorra and the BU629 to Burgos. These hundred odd miles have eased me into riding in Spain. I have stopped to fill up with fuel at a village petrol station with a little bar beside it at Bercedo, and enjoyed the first delicious hit of real Spanish 'café solo' with a juicy chunk of Tortilla and slice of crusty bread. In Burgos I discover that the Plaza Mayor, where I had figured on parking the bike in view of a café table is being ripped up. It has an underground car park underneath and they are 'obra'-ring it good. I have to find my way round to the other side of the cathedral before I find a place to eat in sight of the bike. I have never had anything nicked in Spain, despite using un-lockable soft luggage, but there is always a first time. I visit the castle; one can ride up there, and it has great views across the city and out into the great table-land of the 'meseta'. There is hazy sunshine but a wind is chasing clouds that are not without menace. I head north-east up the Camino de Santiago (N120), the pilgrim way, that trudges to Santiago de Compostela (St James of the field of Stars) from Lourdes and beyond. Even this late in the year at fairly frequent intervals I see 'pilgrims', walkers, staff in hand generally, some with the shell. One of these days I shall do this walk - there are so many great accounts of it painted in so many ways; interestingly many writers seem to have found a mystical element to their journey. Half way between Santo Domingo de la Calzada and Nájera I turn off for Badarán on to the back roads. Map perusal had suggested this round about way to Quintanar; right over the middle of the Sierra. Fairly small by Spanish standards and quite rounded in its older genesis. Still, it rises 6,600 feet. Later I found out what that meant. For now I was happy on minor roads with some sunshine and adventure in the smells of dust and grape harvest. Each little town with the towers or big warehouses of a vineyard gave forth great gusts of the 'must' smell of crushing grapes. In the fields the low, gnarled vines were being searched by hand as the deep blue-black grapes were harvested. Buckets tipped into trailers, piled high they headed for the Vats to put away all this year's hot sun into a bottle of Rioja. I quite quickly leave behind the vineyards as the road begins to climb. After Bobadilla the road becomes the L113 and I come to the doorway to the mountains, a cleft at least a hundred feet deep, guarded by huge near vertical slabs of rock thirty or forty feet thick. The opening is just wide enough for the narrow

road, and a small river. This essentially single-track road winds its way up into the mountains. I flow up as the river flows down. I stop by a small bridge that seems to lead nowhere, there is barely a track on the

This magnificent 14th-century bridge, 32m long and 8.9m high, spans the Najerilla on the old road between the towns of Ventrosa and Anguiano. It was built of ashlars which in posterior repairs have been combined with workstone and rubblework in its upper parts, it represents two round arches of different spans and a central pillar with spillway. The road is paved by smooth stones and the parapets are of rubblework. - So it says on the board by it.

other side. Why was it built? If one followed its open arms where would it lead you? I crunch and slide my way down to the river and wash my face in its cool waters - a ritual more than a refreshment, a private baptism in Spain. On again until I catch the sound of a goat-bell and pull up. I get out my recording equipment (I am gathering material for a radio program) and stalk the goat to capture that, oh so Spanish sound. I get close enough to it. Between scrubby bushes it looks at me with its otherworldly, almond-slitted eyes. There is no sound, it is holding so still its bell is not ringing! A little dance ensues with me trying to get it moving and then stay still myself to get a decent recording. Eventually as a light shower disturbs and darkens the hazy sun so I resume my journey. Now I find more "obras", these works must be to re-surface the road. At present though it just means the surface is strewn with gravel, and gouged by potholes. As a light rain settles in the riding becomes more challenging. When I do pass workmen they stare at me - perhaps they are right; I am 'loco'. The road surface improves but the rain is getting heavier and colder as I climb into the deep timber of the Sierra. Twisting and doubling back on itself, never visible very far ahead, even in good weather; in cloud and rain the desire to push on is tempered by the thought of meeting any traffic, particularly one of those dinosaurian timber lorries that I know lurk in these forests. Higher still, and now the beating rain turns to hammering hail. This is beginning to get a little unpleasant. I have to keep reminding myself of how great it is to be off alone, in Spain. At last the road turns

downward and I think hopefully of the little bar with it's two-headed (stuffed) calf at Huerta de Arriba. A last gauntlet looms from the rain and mist, a herd of horned beasts stands across the road and looks at me without fear, nor intention to give space to get through. I hoot the horn, there is minimal reaction. For the first time on my bike I actually feel rather vulnerable, with trepidation I thread my way through with only feet to spare. Breathing again as

I dodge the slippery traps of rain-soaked cow pats I at last enter the village. I say 'hola' to the dog, and to the Senora in the little bar. Café solo and a plate of aceitunas are my break, the bar is dark as I watch Grandpa trying to keep his granddaughter

amused whilst mother serves me. It is approaching five when I swing through the timber yard that guards the entrance to the campsite at Quintanar. In the UK it would have been called dangerous, the criss-crossing forklifts and huge timber stacks, another 'Way In' would have had to be built. Here it is not even thought of - use your common sense, "esta es"; this is it; it is as it is. A car goes the other way, the driver looking hard at me, I wonder about that. As I ride on, up to the locked gates, my heart sinks. I have soaked gloves and damp boots; what if the site shuts at the end of September? What to do and where to go? The driver of the car returns, he guessed my destination and has turned round to come back and let me in. I ask if the little café will be open for food later, he says yes. I realise the next day that he probably went and arranged for the girl who runs it to open up specially. Robyn from Glasgow (cycled from Madrid) and I are the only customers that dripping evening. I work hard at trying to speak as much Spanish as I can; it is the least one can do in their land and it always pays off. The following day I head onward in search of the Desert of Calanda. Now I am on the N234 and though light drizzle gets more persistent I push steadily east-south-east to Soria and Calatayud. After more than a hundred miles the rain is not just persistent, it is torrential, the lorry-spray a ghastly curtain to be dived through on every overtake. I am losing heart and eventually pull over under the dubious shelter of some trees that are fast heading for nakedness. I switch off and think this through; it does not look any brighter further south and east, there seems very little hope that Calanda will be dry or anything like the deserts of Arizona. It seems like a defeat, but on the other hand; I don't have to do anything I don't want to. I turn round and head back to Burgos, I know the town, I know a good hotel, instead of desert I shall have culture. As I pour water into the basin from my right boot I notice that the sole is flapping loose, the soupy water continues to run as I wring out my gloves. What was that old rhyme about 'the rain in Spain'? The room begins to steam up as the hairdryer stuffed into my glove whines on and on. After a bath I change into dry trousers and rather apprehensively into the battered old baseball boots that I had thought ideal as recreational footwear. I head out into the dripping town, I think I am going to need to increase my wardrobe. Within minutes water has come up through the soles of my shoes and is running down my neck, I buy an umbrella - el paragua. And compose my standard joke of this trip: '¿España es la tierra del sol, No?'; 'Spain is the land of the sun isn't it?' - No, not in October, not in northern Spain. Next day is dry but the weather forecast on the TV showed massed rain clouds and lightning just about everywhere in Spain. I decide to get a bit more culture, relax and enjoy just being here. A pleasant day perambulating the old town and its sites, tracking down a bike shop and buying another pair of gloves and boots to provide spares for my still damp ones. I don't watch the weather forecast for tomorrow, there is not much point as I shall have to make my way over to Jaca whatever the weather. The plan, the 'grand plan' was to be in Jaca one night then a leg to friends just north of Limoges for one night. Then camp somewhere near Cherbourg before catching the morning ferry to Portsmouth. It is quickly dry as I leave Burgos heading eastward, again on the Camino de Santiago. This time on to Logrono and beyond to where I turn from the main road in favour of trying out a cross-country route (NA134). This pays off with some delightful dry, clean and clear roads, swooping over small rises and sinuating away across mile wide, gentle valleys. A great distance of road that can be seen to be completely empty, as are the fields of stubble to either side. This allows me to indulge in riding that one could only otherwise enjoy on a track day. But then you would have other bikes around you. The only spectators for me are the distant heads of the Pyrenees, cloud-hatted but observant to the North. Lodosa, Peralta, Olite and Sangüesa. Onward: I ride the edge of the Embalse de Yesa, against the odd car and occasional bike with whom I exchange salutes. As I draw closer to Jaca I notice that there is a gathering gloom and darkness in my mirrors. When I finally stop on the cobbled streets near a wine store (the obvious reason for stopping). I look back and see an army of cloud, as yet distant on my back trail, but surely advancing steadily. Dark as is the horizon to south and west, to the north seems clearer. The menace of that wet vanguard decides me, I shall

stock up with Rioja and head on into France and perhaps find a dry campsite for the night. Trying to get my bottles into the panniers the side-stand slips and folds up on the uneven cobbles. Over the bike goes before I can do more than vainly strain a muscle to catch it. Petrol is leaking; panic, struggle and strain to get the weight of bike and

very loaded panniers upright. Succeed and then look for damage. Horror!   The clutch lever has been snapped off. Tempered with relief as I realise that a Guzzi man has put a small notch in the lever so that only the top end breaks off; there is enough left to be able to ride. On toward France and a horrendously long tunnel. At first it is fun to hear one's booming exhaust, but as mile after mile of eerily empty, orange

tunnel passes it becomes more and more oppressive and uncanny. I am very relieved finally to see some daylight ahead and to pop out into the real world again. Pau passes and I head up through the forests of the Lande. By early afternoon it seems that I am riding in a slice of sun, to the north dark clouds are gathering. Behind the Pyrenees are lost to me in the darkening haze. I am reaching that point at which it is harder to stop and make a decision than it is to just keep riding. I decide I will try and reach the nearest friendly address; south of Limoges near Jumillhac le Grand live an old school friend's parents. I am sure they won't mind me just turning up; I have visited before. The thought of their hospitality draws me on. On into a chiaroscuro. At one point the western sky is clear and as the sun sets over the unseen, distant sea, a golden wave of light breaks against the black masses of thundercloud spilling toward me from the north. Before the rain reaches me I begin to see the flashes of lightning. Nowhere else have I come across lightning storms like those in this region. I remember some incredible storms in Zululand, but they blew over quickly. Here they seem to circulate, never quite managing to leave the horizon and travel on to other lands. They just return for another go. Soon the rain is pounding me again, the truck spray needing to be continually wiped from my goggles. Around me, in the fields on either side great spikes of unheard lightning splash the road with their glare. At times there are starbursts that break out of the hanging swathes of black clouds. They seem to be reluctant to leave their dark lair though, and like cats-cradles of light claw their way back to the hidden depths of the cloud bank. Releasing so it seems yet more rain. In the gathering gloom of night I no longer try to overtake trucks, despite the spray I am happy to let them light the way ahead and show me where the road is going; easier to follow tail lights at a safe distance than try and read the twisting tarmac that flows out of the darkness. I cannot stop, gone is any real conscious thought of where I am. All I can do is ride on and on, stopping is now an anathema; my focus the immediate one of survival, and the knowledge of an eventual warm and welcoming destination. I finally have to turn off and continue without pathfinder lorries. The back roads to Jumilhac are un-frequented at this time of night. It is 9 pm and I have been riding for 12 hours. The storms have covered the road with leaves and small branches, water-thrown gravel bars and the spiny cases fallen from the chestnut forest's branches that close overhead. In the morning when I see the true state of the roads I travel at half the speed. But for now a 'destination' feels with in reach. I ride on an instinctual level un-hampered by nerves or imagination, I react correctly to every menace and obstacle because I do not waste time thinking about them. With a mile gone I wonder if in the dark I will recognise the farm turning that I rode out of, once, two years ago. Suddenly I do, and make the turn. Down to the end of the track, it seems rather dark. Open the gate and wheel the bike in. My heart sinks as I sense an emptiness in the dark windows. Perhaps they have just gone to bed early or are in a back room, but I know when I knock that the hollowness is real. No one is at home. Of course I should have got in contact before my trip. I remember the woodshed where I put the bike on my last visit. I wheel it in, unload the inside of my tent and finding enough space for it am glad to quickly crawl into a sleeping bag. Thirteen hours of riding, a hard 450 miles plus soon sees me asleep.

In the morning I borrow the garden hose to wash the white froth of chestnut puree from the bike before I set off. It is to be an easy 30 or 40 miles to the next friends, these are at least more or less expecting me, though I had said I would ring from Spain. Unfortunately I had brought the wrong charger for my mobile and left behind my address book, so I have been saving the mobile for emergency use only. A wonderful hearty welcome is mine though, and after days of silence or mangled Spanish it seems almost strange to be carrying on a conversation. After a pleasant lunch I travel on. This day I had planned to see more friends between Rennes and Nantes. Though I had sent a postcard some weeks previously I was not able to follow this up with a phone call. They are not there and so I again spur northward. I feel like I am being reeled in by the long road that is spun out ahead of me and that ends at Cherbourg. As I get closer I start to pass vehicles with English number plates; as these become more common I realise that I might be able to catch a ferry tonight instead of in the morning. This turns out to be the case and I use up the last of my phone battery on a call to my Aunt to see if it will be all right to turn up at 11pm, or later, after the ferry docks. As I claw my way onto the motorway out of Portsmouth I am flashed by another disembarking biker who as he goes past points at my rear tyre. I pull over on the hard shoulder to look. Tyre is all right, then 'oh bother' I have no tail light. Well I have no intention of trying to fix that in the dark on the rain and spray-covered motorway edge. I decide to ride hard the rest of the thirty miles to my Aunt's. If I am careful no car will be going fast enough to come up behind me, if they do I will either lightly touch the brakes and or indicate. I am probably lucky not to get stopped by the police, but it is a filthy night. When I finally climb off the bike outside her cottage it has been another 13 hours of travel.

Next day I finally swing down the bends of the A44 from the Eisteddfa Gurig watershed. I am drawn home, like the water of the streams that now cannot escape the ruler-like line of the sea that underlines the horizon. It does not seem possible that only 8 days have passed since I rode up these sweeps. But I am coming back a changed and invigorated man. I am tired and damp, but I have been to see the elephant (as they used to say in the Old, and Wild West).

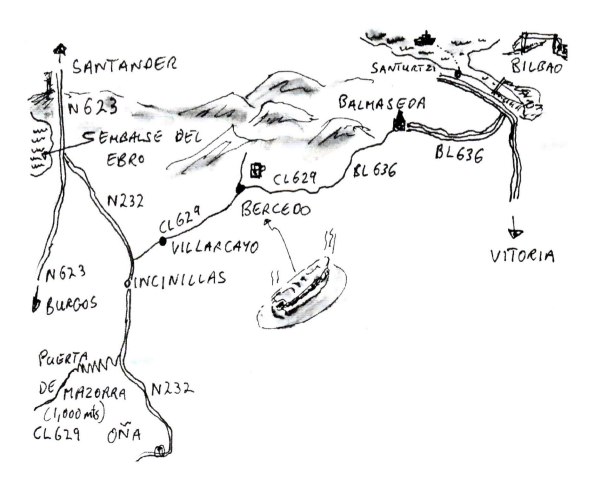

THE ADVENTURES OF
DON DUNCAN. 2004

"*Somewhere in La Mancha, in a place whose name I do not care to remember, a gentleman...*"

Pulls his horse to a roadside stop, ground hitches her and slowly removes his helmet. Across the skyline march an army of enormous giants, each sedately wheeling their three arms in menacing gestures of defiance.

It is good to stop. Take a deep breath of the thick hot air of Spain, like a tasty chunk of chorizo it assaults your senses with strength and subtlety. The sharp tang of verge-heated wild herbs overlays the dust kicked up by my horse's hooves as we left the tarmac and came to rest on the rutted dirt of the hard shoulder. Unhurriedly I remove my gloves and jacket. As I drop them across my 'Rocinante's' seat I feel a year's worth of busy-ness and stress begin to slide from me, alongside the thin trickles of sweat that start as the great August sky of Spain settles over me.

Alone at last. After a year of fighting many armed giants and warlocks, I am at last free. Do you find biking brings inner space? I think the very act of setting off from your front door on a motorbike brings on whispers of romance and legend. You may deny it, but deep down, buried away with your childhood dreams there is an echo of the Lone Ranger, Robin Hood, Richard the Lionheart... Do you not feel a certain elitism, a difference from those 'others' in their cars? Why is there so much difference between driving a car and riding a bike? Does it lie in the greater immediacy of control, the sense of far greater interaction with the physical forces propelling you? And though you may hedge the question with family and loved ones; there is an inherent level of danger. In fact do not the whispers of fear for your safety feed your own sense of bravery? I go where others fear, I do what others won't. Is not an essential part of the buzz, the act of beating down those foes and fears, whether imaginary or real. Last year my research trip to a Spanish desert ended in ignominious retreat and wash out. Now in mid-August I have ten whole days, time and weather to reach the 'Western' film sets of Almeria. 'Ahora' (now). Here. On my first day back in Spain, I feel a great release. I've made it, made it back here, but more than that; I have again beaten down the craven worries, been victorious over the planning and booking. 'Ahora mismo', I am alone, abroad, and ahead of me stretch the great plains of La Mancha - of all Spain. Riddled with giants and errant Knights, and probably some very errant (not that I'd have anything to do with them) Ladies. I have left behind my 'Dulcinea of Toboso'. The Lady of my thoughts, in far Aberystwyth and now, as a true knight must, I shall re-mount and carry forward my lance in search of adventure...

Doesn't sound quite the same somehow; "Lucy of Aberystwyth". Anyway... Come 'Rocinante', or rather 'Veloz' to be true to my steed. We must leave these giants to their endless toil and ride onward...

The first test of my knighthood had come as I swung the bends of the A470, bent by the course of the now summer-quieted River Wye. At around sixty I saw a bullet coming straight for me. Perhaps if you ride with a full-face you have not had this experience. It is a cartoon moment in which time is slowed and awareness is instantaneous though reaction impossible, (and generally not advisable) just spend those instants bracing for the impact! The wasp hit me in the middle of my forehead above my shades, the impact was briefly numbing before I realised that the little swine had managed to somehow sting me in the instant it mashed! Arriving at Portsmouth (complete with bindi) I find that the boat has been delayed; could this be due to Hurricane Alex who had rather carelessly wandered over our side of the pond, and needlessly given ammunition for various people's happy asides about the reputation of crossing the Bay of Biscay. 'Technical problems' are the trouble apparently. What sort of? "Lost an engine." Hmm, careless; bit difficult one might have thought. Waiting to board one meets other two-wheeled adventurers, and soon by some sort of alchemy you find those with the most in common, in outlook if not in choice of steed. Cor and Jude ride a Harley Davidson, but we still make friends...

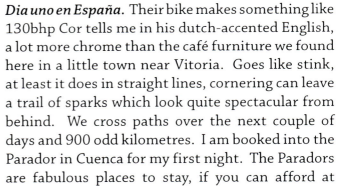

Dia uno en España. Their bike makes something like 130bhp Cor tells me in his dutch-accented English, a lot more chrome than the café furniture we found here in a little town near Vitoria. Goes like stink, at least it does in straight lines, cornering can leave a trail of sparks which look quite spectacular from behind. We cross paths over the next couple of days and 900 odd kilometres. I am booked into the Parador in Cuenca for my first night. The Paradors are fabulous places to stay, if you can afford at

The Parador at Cuenca from the castle which is above the town and across the gorge. The courtyard in the middle is shown up by the trees growing out of it. There is a footbridge high over the gorge to the famous 'hanging houses' built out on the cliff edge. One of which houses an Art Gallery and also a restaurant. There is Cathedral to see and many winding old streets to enjoy. The Panorama below was taken from the front of the Parador.

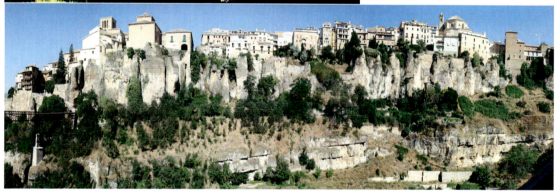

least one night in a trip, do so. The buildings are nearly always beautifully done up monasteries or the like. The décor, rooms, everything is of an extremely high standard, you get three times what you would get from a UK Hotel for that price. I roll into gorge-split Cuenca, with its 'hanging houses', after a pretty easy 550 km from Bilbao. I have at times taken a less back-road route than I had planned as Cor and Jude's bike didn't really agree with lumpy and twisty roads. That is until we parted at Molina de Aragon from where I took a typically expansive and diverse back road for Cuenca. Gorges, tiny villages, dusty fields and the great blue sky, rushing rivers and ancient monuments as I traverse the Montes de Picaza. Yet again I appreciate the great flexibility of the Centauro. On the Autovia I rest my chest on the tank-bag and set the wrist-twist to a comfortable cruising speed. Get off that boring ruler and find some 'A' style roads. In Spain where an 'N' road has been usurped by a new Autovia you can guarantee a better ride on the old road which has lost all but sporadic local traffic. The Autovia is like a river, man-constrained by levees and dikes, uniform in bend, width and speed of flow. The 'N' road is a meandering river that flows into the pools of little towns and there swirls about a bit before carrying you on again. The changes in pace and sights, sounds and smells that result help to break one out of that 'get there' travel attitude. Now you've eased up a bit why not be a bit more daring; see if on the map you can find a direct line of little white and yellow roads that will connect you to your next town. It won't always be easy; a couple of times I went round and round inside a small village, much to the much-saluted old men's interest. The stream of the road having lost its integrity, spreading out to trickle all around the obstruction of 30 houses. Carrying a compass on the tank-bag can help here to give one an idea of which direction in which to break out. Here, on often single track roads with lorry-rumpled corners, livestock and hidden bends, you might think the Centauro would lose its feet. But it doesn't, those Brembos can haul even the loaded bike up in a remarkably short and safe time. The suspension handles what the road throws at it without complaint and he doesn't wag his head or rear up in distress. The worst I rode was on the southern side of the Duero from Toro, headed into Zamora. It was like a washboard, with holes in, and I doubt there are that many bikes that could have handled it much better; a cruiser would have grounded out and a sports or sports-tourer would probably have twitched its rider into the ditch, which was quite deep!

Dia dos en España.   I head out of Cuenca bound for the 'Ciudad Encantada', its name made it a must see ('Enchanted City'). I have to say that though it was very interesting and at times bizarre, it was not really what I had expected. A maze of weather-riven rocks with sometimes appropriate but often rather hopeful names. Mar de Piedra, El Teatro, El Diplodocus, Cara del Hombre, El Perro and others. A sniff of Don Quixote I think. He would surely have never got out of here in one piece, his rampant (quixotic) imagination would have driven him into yet more terribly one-sided battles with the likes of El Cocodrillo y El Elefante. As it was I had one of those interludes that are so much a part of touring on your own. A New Zealand couple who gave me a cup of coffee and with whom I chatted as we went around the Ciudad. We parted never to meet again, but all enriched. At this point I was without a definite itinerary, I had deliberately organised few fixed points, (booked Hotel/ Parador) so that although I had an idea where I would be each of my nights, I was free to change direction at a whim. For me this is an important part of the lone knight's quest. As Don Quixote sets out with only the certainty of adventure happening, and a total acceptance of what will be will be... Qué sera, sera! So launch yourself out into the wider world of mañana, and what might or might not happen, and relish whatever does. Taking a white road off the N320 to skirt Albacete (seen it before) via La Roda I stop to bite on a hunk of bread and gnaw the end off a chorizo sausage. I get a text from Jude, upshot I switch direction and head for a rendezvous in Almansa, a ninety degree change of course! Looking at the map I see the CM3218, a striking rattler if ever there was one - clinging the edges of the Rio Jucar. If the road has that many bends showing on a 1/400 000 map in Spain it is going to be MAJORLY wiggly! It is. A stupendous snaking ride, often down to first gear to ride blind, tight corners

under flood-gutted overhangs on a road barely wide enough for four wheels. Bursting out into hot sunshine after the shadowed Rivendell of the cañón I pull over to check the map and throw off my jacket, and top up my water levels. My Gialli denim jacket is generally cool; it will wick away sweat and yet gives some protection. For me an acceptable compromise between brain-sapping discomfort and the idiocy of the topless rider. Jeans on the bottom half with 'hi-protect' and knee padding complete this knight's armour. One of the most important things in these temperatures is taking on enough water; the wind itself will strip you of moisture without you

noticing. Think about it; you could dry a washed 'T' shirt in half an hour! Two Guardia Civil in a car roll pass looking bemused at this, out of place 'extranjero'. They cruise on toward Alcalá del Jucar where the map says there is a bullring, I can't figure where, as we seem to be at the bottom of a three hundred foot canyon. Anyway I know where I am and hang a right up a twisting road-cut, with 16m solid rock walls to either side; the contained heat is a solid force, I love it. Out of the cañón I traverse a very apposite 'mountain'; the Sierra de la Caballa. Although a first glance into the dictionary comes up with 'mackerel' I'm sure that it must refer to the horse (caballar), the gentleman or knight (caballero) and the 'caballista' (good rider) or even cabalistico (occult). Cresting three thousand feet I canter down the CM3201 toward Almansa. Here after a certain amount of 'aquí para allá', (to and fro) on our mobiles we meet under the impressive rock-crested castle.   Where does one draw the line in today's technological wonderland? What's the difference between a mobile phone, a digital camera and a GPS system? I can only respond for myself. Para mi, a GPS is one step too far, I want to be able to make mistakes, to get it wrong, and then get myself out of it, or more often than not just take the new direction, enjoy it, live it, love what turns up with the added blessing of the frisson of the unexpected. Once you've plotted in a course, are you going to change it? A mobile now seems common sense, in case of an accident. I have at least 'tres veces' (three times) called the emergency services to accidents I have come across. The digital camera is, I admit, laziness. It is easier to load onto the computer when I get home. However I still carry my trusty Canon A1 SLR to take the really important shots. With Cor and Jude I ride to Yecla where we find the delightful Hotel Avenida, nice rooms, good price, in the middle of town (right out the door and 30 metres down on the left for a great meal). Best of all a lock up garage with direct access to the rooms.

Dia tres. I take a fabulously mad route to Tabernas, close to 'Mini-Hollywood', the goal of the trip. Michelin say the shortest route is around 240 km, I manage to notch up nearly 480 this day. Not all of it intentional. I had tried to pre-book the Hospederia del Desierto (very close to the Almeria racing circuit), but had been told it wasn't possible. For some reason I thought they were probably just being cautious and that when I got there they would find me something. No such luck! It's a special Saturday for getting married. Anywhere to camp? Nada. So I somewhat tiredly and forlornly headed back onto the road. Reaching Tabernas itself I saw from the road a sign painted on a building 'HOTEL'. It didn't look too promising but after a trip round the village that showed no other candidates I drew up and tried the door. After a while I was shown to a very small room. Oh well, it's an experience, take what comes. After attempting a shower, (broken) like the rather smelly toilet, I lie down for a rest. Now I find myself being eaten by small but extremely aggressive biting flies. Enough is enough, I'd rather sleep in a ditch. I quickly pack, make vague excuses, and leg it! 100 odd kilometres later as full-dark settles across the Mediterranean I am putting my tent up on the beach north of Carbonares.

Can I write a novel that people will buy? How much use is a film set in Spain going to be to Arizona 1870? Am I not like Don Quixote, living in a fantasy of my own making? But then the essence of being human is that each of us lives our own particular world. Two people travelling the same road at the same time in the same way will experience it differently. Ewan and Charlie bike round the World, but is their adventure any more adventurous than mine? I think one must live to one's own expectation and not borrow from someone else's. I prefer riding alone most of the time. I alone am pushing myself forward into new experiences and must not falter

from my vision or I will find like Don Quixote that some wizard has changed my battling armies into a herd of sheep.

Dia cuatro.

So today I visit 'Mini-Hollywood' and 'Fort Bravo'. Both somewhat odd collections of bits of Western townships. The trouble is the difficulty of separating the film 'truth' from what the reality actually was. It's all good fun though; actors stroll around and look mean etc and eventually act out a scenario of bank robbery, pursuit, capture and a hanging. Lots of blanks being fired and horses cantered. Moving on to the second film set (Fort Bravo) which I found more interesting with its Mexican pueblo section, I find some of the same actors and a very similar scenario. The good bit was tasting the horse-kicked-up dust as it swirled into my face. Feeling the heat of the sun as it flensed the greying timbers of the clapboard buildings and brought me the pungent smell of horse sweat, the creak of saddle and snort of horse. I feel through the tourist coating a brief touch of a time gone. A time I am feebly trying to live in, my own way, in my novel Mogollon Gold. I can now get a room in the Hostal Calatrava (25€), part of the Hospederia del Desierto. It is now deserted of wedding guests. This night I find pieces of my novel echoing down my dreams.

"The *pile of boulders seemed indifferent and insignificant against the backdrop of the river beyond. Within the nest of rocks there was a bowl-shaped space scarce 20' across with a bit of dusty, drying grass and the merest hint of a seep of water. In the sandy run between two large rocks a small hot fire was busy heating a coffee pot and a pan of broiling meat. The fire was made with ironwood and mesquite and made hardly any smoke. The mouth-watering smells of broiling meat and coffee seemed a danger worth risking to the lean young man who occasionally poked the meat around in the pan. His eyes frequently flicked to the line-backed dun horse that contentedly cropped the dry grass, seeming to find it fine fare. If anything living drew near he knew the horse would know it first. There was some danger in stopping here for food and rest, but he was tired of running. Tonight he would enjoy his food and the clear, still, starlit night to come. Tomorrow if they wanted trouble they could buy it in full measure!"*

Dia cinco. Today was the ride of the whole trip. Exhausting, exhilarating, seemingly endless. Somehow the day seemed to stretch itself as I rode, to encompass the distance covered. A distance not only measured in turns of my wheels but also in both history and geography. A journey from the Moorish, 'african' landscape of the Almeria desert, beating north and west against the receding tide of the Moorish conquest and ending in the mist-soaked Sierra de Gredos (100+ kilometres from Madrid), from which the God-armed Christian knights imposed the Reconquista. First of all the road to Granada, over 140 km of sweeping hot tarmac and exploding views of the Sierra Nevada (mountains of snow) reaching up to 9,000' and holding high the most southerly permanent snow in Europe. I eventually manage to spot a small dirty white area that I decide is my glimpse of that snow. Coming round a long bend after passing the Puerta Lobo (wolf-pass) I find the city spread out before me in the distance, I eagerly look for any sign of La Alhambra, the fabled Moorish citadel of many awed descriptions. When I finally find it I can see nothing but a long low red-brown wall. And it is fully-booked! They only allow a certain number in at any time in order to preserve something of its fabled magic. Book in advance is the answer. Next great Spanish city on the list is Cordoba about 160 km. 50 odd kilometres later I pass through Alcalá, unfortunately 3 months before reading the wonderful book by Michael Jacobs - 'The Factory of Light', which is set in the tiny nearby village of Frailes. I would have eagerly gone to visit. His invocation of the magical and the tawdry side of Spain, clearly seen though, through a definite sense of love, warmed up my dull November.

In Cordoba I pull off onto a wide pavement close to the river, within sight of the great Cathedral - La Mesquita. Across the road an inviting café where I 'café solo' up and eat a 'cacho'. When I ask the owner if my bike will be safe where it is, across the road, whilst I go to the Mesquita, she tells me to bring it over in front of her café, she will keep an eye on it for me. So typical of the openness and helpfulness a little effort with language brings. Though I took rather pathetic little padlocks (one yank and they'd break) in a sop to protecting my gear in its soft Oxford bags, no-one ever even tried to get into them. I think a bit of common sense about where you leave your bike is worth more than any expensive hard, locking kit. Yes, a risk, but I'm happy to take it. Many would say the Centauro was not a 'tourer', that it lacks protection from the weather, is only 'Guzzi'-smooth (a relative term). I believe it's a brilliant tourer, and stuff all those Bike magazines that try and tell me what I should be riding. Perhaps this is because in my 'quixotic' world I am at moments riding a horse with saddle-bags slung. Sometimes in armour, jousting with thundering pantechnicons, at others I ride the wild west of my imagination, holding the reins with one hand I rest my other close to my left gun butt as I ride into town. As we who are privileged to ride them know, our Guzzi horses are individualists like us, not perfect, needing some care and a certain kind of handling. Read 'Spanish Steps' by Tim Moore; he might be riding a donkey but he is riding with a character and that is what we do. Biking is an individualist's sport: always take your own camino! The Mezquita was wonderful, all those Arabic arches and tiled floors, a mosque turned into a cathedral but without destroying the Moorish spirit which

I felt still dwelt there in the blood red stones. The Christians may have thrown out (so they say) all the Arabs, but in truth in physical form and colouring, in the many facets of their community and society the Moorish blood and life lives on, quietly hidden in the very sinews of Spain.

I head north out of Cordoba, for a while on the road to Badajoz; I would love to fit it in as well, but the days are passing inexorably toward that return ferry. After 50 km I turn off onto the back roads and for 250 km wind through a changing land, the vast dryness and expanses of Andalusia giving gradual way to the more intricate and varied lands of Extremadura. Mountains and embalses (reservoirs), villages seeming lost in time and the looping road that shuns their donkey-wide streets. At Belalcázar I

pull over to photograph one of those unexpected 'moments, vistas' that occur whenever you take the back roads. After 50km of windswept, open and sometimes rocky land the road by-passes yet another white village tightly wrapped around a small hilltop. I think nothing of it, till as I pass it by a monumental

castellation looms into view, it seems much bigger than the village though it shows no signs of life. The architecture is very unusual; what is Moorish, what gothic, did it start as a monastery or a grain store? Olive trees advance like a spreading army to lay siege, and are dwarfed by the vast central keep. And then between me and the castle I see the rearguard of the assault that has conquered. A series of tractor sheds

engulfed in a bizarre jumble of machinery and trash, the tin roofs held down with stones, probably originally from the castles outer works. Veloz and I must be away, away to cross the Rio Zujar and onward into the mysterious lands of Extremadura. The part of Spain that is forgotten, the idiot child forever ostracised from the fire of Andalucia and the aristocracy of Castille. Extremadura seems without the nationalism or champions of the Catalans or Basques. But it is always there, has always been there, quietly working its high rocky way along the backbone of Iberia.

This is where I love my Centauro; after countless hours riding everything from motorway to single track pothole, together we swing on, the big 'V' heart beating a constant rhythm that infuses me; I beat to the same tempo. I don't think my riding, I don't anticipate our moves. We just do it together. Sometimes on a long straight we rear up. Kick heels and wind forward riding the great surge of speed and torque. Having been loping along in top at 2-3,000 rpm we are now winding on to 6,000 and the speedo heads for the ton. The next vista opens up, and I ease the throttle, the thrumming slowing to a lazy beat as I watch a Booted Eagle slipping across the sky. Now as we ride the wild lands where rocks like sharks surfacing, cut free through the dry dead grass of a parched upland, a wind begins to blow. At first I hardly notice it but coming up onto an open plain I find I am having to ride canted over to one side. Travel becomes more physical as I cross the Sierra de Guadalupe towards Talavera de la Reina. North of Talavera the next mountain range, the Sierra de Gredos, (over 8,000') is gathering a dark cloak of steel and iron clouds. The miles still pass. Mucho viento! Y ahora llueve. There are big roadworks near Talavera, I stop in a bar where a 'muy bien' senorita serves me with chunks of tasty meat, rice and juicy tortilla, water and café solo. The length of country is now telling. The day wanes in concert with my eventual tiring and getting started again needs a laying of spurs to the flanks of my will. Crossing the Rio Guadyerbas and Tietar we head upward into La Gredos and its rainy cloak. North of Arenas at Mombeltrán, as the light fades, I see a sign for a Hostal and camping. Without a moments doubt I head for it. Now, after all these miles I am stiffened, though mostly by the wind. My welcome is genuine, yes, a room (I couldn't face getting the tent set up), yes, you can put your Moto under the little outside roof where the kids are laughing over an old table-football game. And when settled and back at the bar there is free tapas with the schooner of beer the barman fixes me. A simple, but unbelievably satisfying tortilla and 'pan' supper. Well over 700 km and I am ready for bed! As I head for the land of nod I unwind again that skein of tarmac, it seems days ago that I left the Hostal at Tabernas amid the 100°+ desierto. So many sights and smells that will mostly fade in the coming days, leaving only a glorious aftertaste.

Dia seis. In the morning a light mist, which comes and goes as I climb towards the pass of the Puerto del Pico (4,437') where for a while it drizzles. At first I am irritated, and riding rather gingerly, but then as the clouds part I gain magnificent views of the mountains and it all makes sense. Without the blindfold of cloud I couldn't have had the sudden revelation. Without times of riding wet and cold there would be less joy on a dry day. Ahora mismo on the twisting mountain road, the dampness seems to accentuate the heady scents of pine and rosemary, which along with broom clothe what I can see of the roadsides. The road criss-crosses and cuts through long paved and sloping steps which I realise are remains of a Roman road; in the mist I imagine the legions marching, the length of each 4 or 5 meter 'step' probably carefully engineered to suit their marching rhythm. Next I pass over the Sierra de Villafranca through the Puerto de la Peña Negra 1909m (6,263'). Up here I am in thick cloud with visibility down to yards, however as I wind my way down I drop suddenly clear and find a huge swathe of country in bright sun, textured by the shadows of drifting clouds.

A Red Kite gracefully drifts across the scene and I am transported back home to my kitchen where hangs a Michael Ayrton etching that is this scene. Uncanny. I hurry on down flitting left and right to the beating pace of the road's hairpins. A bird flits across in front of me, dazzling me with flashes of blue, green and tawny red. I slam on the brakes and rip off my helmet, almost dropping the bike in my hurry to get at my binoculars. First I am aware of the penetrating, purring, chirruping calls, and then the fast flying shapes are a flock of twenty or more Bee-eaters, all around me their jewel-like colours shimmer. I take off my jacket and fling it on the bike, soak up the sun to dispel the last vestiges of the cold heights of the Sierra and fill my heart with that thrilling, trilling sound and sight. To ice the ornithological cake; as I am re-armouring myself a huge Black Vulture drifts across the face of the mountains. In Piedrahita I have trouble getting through the town; most roads are closed and all are thronged with people in their best clothes. A fiesta for sure. I am sorely tempted to stop and join in, but really I need to make Salamanca in time to find a campsite and see the city as I am expected in Zamora mañana. I am blown into Salamanca by a bruising wind but manage to find a good campsite at the Hotel Regio. After putting up my tent I find I can catch a bus from the hotel Car Park to the city centre. A short walk through the back streets and I find my way to the

Panorama approaching the Miajes pass from the south - Sierra de Gredos

grand central square, the Plaza Mayor. It is great to sit with a glass of wine in this great space, with only the muted sounds of conversation rustling through it like dry leaves, the traffic that lays siege cannot do more than sound the odd horn from beyond the ramparts. Salamanca is truly a city of golden stone. The Cathedral in its gothic splendour a huge contrast to Moorish Cordoba. Having walked a few of the sights I return to the plaza for another glass of wine. A warm ray of sunshine gets through the clouds and past the circling Storks. Perhaps a hundred or more are drifting across the sky, aimlessly criss-crossing the city. After a blustery night and with uncertain weather I head north once more for Zamora. The direct road is 60 km, I manage to turn this into over 130, including the aforementioned 'track' across the river from Toro. I arrive in Zamora in a soaking, driving rain that somehow washes me up outside the Parador. Various intentions of camping or cheap hostelling go out of the window and I book in. Luxury, luxury, luxury! By now my Spanish is improving no end; it seems that when I have it all around me it permeates my brain and suddenly I find a vocabulary that I can never find at home. It is a great feeling to be able to carry on something approaching a conversation and be able to answer more than the most basic questions. This was

all put to the test when I met up with old friends of my father's. Though they had some English it was as rusty as my Spanish. However through the next three days of wonderful hospitality and discussion we all improved linguistically. They pass in a wonderful meaty stew of mangled Spanish and English, architecture and restaurants, remembrance of my father and discussions of all manner of things.

Dia siete - ocho. Zamora is a smaller city than Salamanca, the plain sister, less busy and touristy but friendlier, more intimate. We visit Toro which is a small town

set on a bluff over-looking the Duero. Here my Spanish is forced into overdrive by meetings with many relations and acquaintances. Like my father, Manuel is always ready to sketch and always ready to get into conversation. One evening we visited an amazing underground Bodega. On the outskirts of a nondescript village there is an area of criss-crossing sandy tracks, between them low mounds and odd little brick chimneys jutting from the ground. Here and there, are what look like small brick sheds, each with a single door. Entering one of these you descend by a narrow stairway, deep into the ground. At least thirty or forty feet I would guess. At the bottom there is a charcoal fire for cooking delicious local food and a simple bar from which a rough and ready jar of wine is available. Don't try it if you are claustrophobic or worried about the Health and Safety aspects.

Another time they drive me to Miranda de Duero in Portugal where I sample a fantastic baccalao - salted cod, that melts in the mouth.

Huerta de Arriba. 8/09

Sadly I eventually have to move on to Burgos, where I have two nights booked, and paid for over the internet. Note although this means you know you've got a bed and you can get good price deals, the drawback is you can't get a refund off the Hotel if you cancel all or part of the stay.

Dia nueve - diez. Back in my old stamping grounds I enjoy my usual round of sights and pay a visit to Huerta de Arriba. Sitting outside the bar sketching with a beer and a plate of olives I get many complimentary remarks and some nice conversation. In another little village, Huérmeces, outside the bar as we wait for it to open, I meet a French hunter and a Spanish cyclist. I hear the thrum of dramatic guitar chords and see... The Good, the Bad, and the Ugly! Naturally I am the Good and I guess the hunter is the Bad, certainly cyclist wear is pretty ghastly.

I enjoy the evenings by the river in Burgos enjoying the paseo and the music of the fountains under the deep green canopy of the plane trees.

Dia once. Finally my last morning in Spain dawned. An easy cross-country run to Bilbao and suddenly I am back speaking English as I join other bikers waiting to embark. Some are those briefly met on the way out, including one who had asked for my advice on routes along the Pyrenees, and now was delighted to tell me how he had completely ignored my suggestions. His wife never did look all that happy.

Cuviers Beaked, Fin and Minke (possibly a Sperm) Whale enliven the return trip and compensate for saying 'adios' to Spain. Or rather 'hasta luego' for I shall surely be back.

A round trip of nearly 6,500 km (4,000 miles), including the sea crossings. The memories and experience mirroring the trip, some events seem to speed by, flashes of encapsulated moments that have flown free of the blurring passage of miles. Others are there to savour, long and sensual. The bad moments; being eaten alive in that crummy Hotel, blown sideways by unrelenting wind, frustration at my inability to communicate adequately.

These are the salt and pepper, the darkness and pain, that allow the light to blaze out.

Hasta la próxima vez en España!

A view of the Rio Jucar canyon.

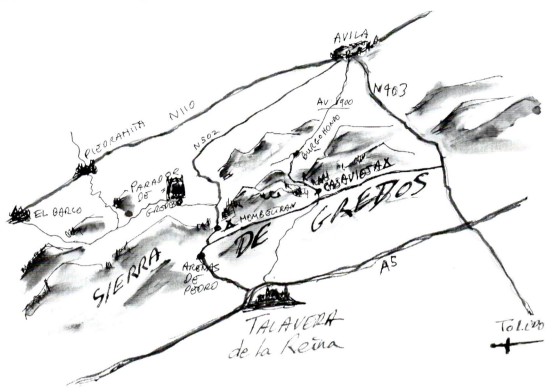

At the end of the Rio Jucar is Alcala. In the canon wall you can see the windows of houses and a restaurant - Cuevas de Diablo!

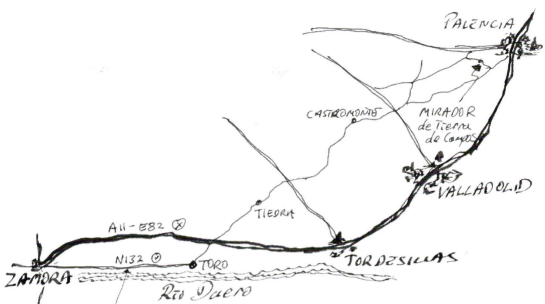

"Somewhere in La Mancha, in a place whose name I do not care to remember, a gentleman..." In case you didn't guess, is the opening line from 'Don Quixote' by Cervantes. It is a *big* read, but if you persevere and start seeing the humour it is very funny, you can recognise characters around you today. It is actually a very, very important book 'literally', in many ways a foundation of modern fiction. 1605!

Mirador de la Tierra de Campos near Palencia

In the Rio Jucar canyon.

2005

The two have always gone together for me. Of course one does have to do the pedestrian bit in order to get really close, but quite a few of my most satisfactory 'on the wing' events have come from my bike. This year my 'reason' for going to Spain was photographic. I am busy (between busy) putting together a book of my Spanish travels and biking articles and needed more photos of roads and places - cast iron! Away to go; I tried a different ferry crossing, partly due to timing the departure to fit in with my 'free time' slot. Portsmouth - St Malo overnight, not as cheap as going to Cherbourg but arriving a hundred miles or so further south. As always worth taking supper and a drink on board if you want to save twenty quid. A quick birdless blast to Derval and old friends; I had planned on being on my way again within a few hours, but three donkeys and an armoured Bentley intervened (the donkeys needed feeding, and the unique, Diplomatic Corps plated car needed photographing). I only set off again the following morning. Now I was a day behind and despite my intention to take it slower through France and try and find interesting and bendy back roads I ended up doing a long distance blast all the way over the Pyrenees into Spain ending in Jaca. 10 hours 465 miles. Not a lot of time for birds though a few of those spirit-lifting moments, a soaring Buzzard, hovering Windhover or the quick glimpse of a hunting Hen Harrier. And as soon as the Mountains rose up at the end of the Lande I was on the look out for the great shapes of the Griffon Vulture ('flying doors'), the wings so broad and long that at a distance the head and tail are hardly noticeable. It

is why raptor watching works well with biking; the birds are up in the clear air, often soaring relatively slowly and they are big as well and so easy to spot. As they drift upward on a thermal one often has time to find a space to stop and pull out the binoculars before they are out of sight.

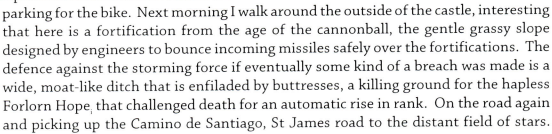

A pleasant Hostal in Jaca with secure parking for the bike. Next morning I walk around the outside of the castle, interesting that here is a fortification from the age of the cannonball, the gentle grassy slope designed by engineers to bounce incoming missiles safely over the fortifications. The defence against the storming force if eventually some kind of a breach was made is a wide, moat-like ditch that is enfiladed by buttresses, a killing ground for the hapless Forlorn Hope, that challenged death for an automatic rise in rank. On the road again and picking up the Camino de Santiago, St James road to the distant field of stars.

A landfill site I come across is a magnet for vultures and I have a close view of an Egyptian Vulture as well as the Red Kites that are about as common here as they are now back home in Wales. Swinging past the Embalse de Yesa one can see the effects of the dry summer. In Olite I come across a fantastic confection of castellation, at first I suspect the Parador but seeing this further on I guess it was just another of the myriad castles of Castilla. This one crenellated and vertical, a roost for archers and the throwers of boiling oil, its fancy walls would have been pounded to rubble within a day by artillery of any strength. It is along this stretch that a previous year I had a wonderful view of a Bearded Vulture, the Lammergeyer of bone-dropping tales. It was gliding roughly parallel with the road and so with fairly frequent attention to the mundane tarmac I could enjoy it's effortless, glide beside me and see it's tasselled moustache. I can see that you will say that the practice of bird watching whilst riding a motorbike is one of extreme foolhardiness. It certainly could be, if one was to lose a sense of priority.

But given my ornithological bent I see it as a fairly natural extension of that awareness and constant searching gaze, from near to far that is the backbone of safe riding. One scans far ahead for signs of the road's future passage and potential dangers, so keeping a sharp anticipation of avian wonders keeps the eyes focus wide... Now I swing into my little mountain range, the Sierra de la Demanda. Leave behind the 'staff and scallop shell' bearing pilgrims and plunge through the doorway of Adriano into the crevices of the river Najera. At first I relish the newly surfaced road that has replaced the potholed and gravel strewn track of two years before. Though faster and easier on the mind it is still not a road to let the mind or eye wander as bend follows bend, some shallow some very sharp, some with warning signs, some without. Here Red-footed Falcons could be playing the updrafts from the cliffs that hang over the road and I wouldn't see them. But stop at the 14thC 'bridge to nowhere' and whilst the bike ticks and tocks to itself one lets in first the quietness - absence of wind and engine, and then as ears adjust, begin to listen to the garrulous Spanish of the river gossiping its way over boulders and tripping over the extended legs of stunted waterside birches. No great burst of bird song here but after a while one becomes aware of furtive movements, of accentor warning clacks. If one wants to walk a while one may see the Blue Rock Thrush, though at this hot time of day most of the small birds are brush and shade-bound. In the narrow cleft of sky above one can catch the dots of distant Buzzards and Kites or perhaps again the vast, patient, flap and glide of Griffons. There are so many in these mountains I find it hard to understand how they can find enough carrion to live on. But then this country hides many of its secrets in the dark of night or the faint, first light that coolly glistens over the shadowed gorges. Saddle the horse again, within a few miles the road suddenly resumes the condition I remember, as if tired of being smartly dressed and rather liking to drop its gravel on the corners and spit out potholes and irregular lumps and bumps. To the Quintanar campsite where constant Grey and Pied Wagtails flick their tails along the small, tamed river that runs through the middle of the site. The Sparrows and Robins are sharp now the August hordes of holidaying Spaniards have left. One Dutch caravan and this noisily burbling motorbike are the only possible providers of crumbs. Big Mistle Thrushes though are happy to hunt the clear dusty ground. And in the pine trees there is the happy song of Serins at the pine cones, they don't care who is underneath, though the Great-Spotted Woodpecker sounds annoyed as he peers carefully from behind a dead branch. The restaurant is open so a meal is not hard to find, a bottle of good rough vino tinto washes it down. I have brought my S.A.S. jungle sleeping bag which very nicely packs up to barely 8" square. Unfortunately as darkness falls I begin to wonder if it was a wise choice; within a couple of hours I know it wasn't, all spare clothing is draped around my attempted cocoon of warmth that is being teased away by an insidious chill that deepens and

hardens as the long night wears on, and on. Snatched minutes of sleep follow frantic rearrangement of the patchwork that seems to be incapable of staying complete. In the morning as I clasp two cups of harsh instant espresso from the 24hr machine the cheery Dutchman tells me the temperature was down to at least 0°. I shiver and concur, pack up as my warming limbs allow and head onward looking for a warm sunny spot to really gather some heat.

I find a nice one near Salas de las Infantes. I can watch the Griffons who have also spent a cold night, fumble off their rocky ledges, spilling downward till they catch the first thermals of the day and lift away to search for any night accidents. On to a favourite little village that from one side is reached by the flat stubble lands that write La Mancha large across the meseta; from the other side you have come through a winding river-threaded gorge lush with trees and tangled growth where small LBJ's (Little Brown Jobs) abound. I stop and finding a good parking space off the road for the bike, scramble up the rocky hillside till I can see the village peeping through my craggy doorway. I sit to sketch and become aware of big eagles riding the cliff

updrafts; studying them I realise with a thrill that they are Golden Eagles. One starts to display, gaining height and then folding in his wings and dropping like a cannonball towards the baking ground before with a subtle change of wing hurtling skyward again in a parabola that has me straining in sympathy with the 'g' forces. Here also are Choughs that cough and cry

shrill as they wheel in annoyance at the Eagles' trespass. I studiously drink my litre of water as thin lines of sweat quickly dry upon my back. The chorus of crickets and cicadas begins to grow in intensity with the heat reflected from the boulders around me. The smell of rock and crushed wild herbs salute the growing heat of midday. I am looking forward to a nice lunch in the village bar, but when I get there it is shut. After being investigated by an old lady-watchdog I learn that the bar owner has gone away for his annual holiday. As the week progresses I realise that in the smaller communities this is very common. Of course in August comes the influx of family that have moved to the cities to work and so there is constant business, but now in September it is the bar owners turn to vacate for vacation.   A periodic check of the bike and I realise that the blast through France has worn out my back tyre. With memories of going through to stitching in 150 miles I have to address the task of finding a bike shop. Luckily the very nice Hostal I am staying at in Burgos has a very pleasant and helpful brother and sister with excellent English. They are more than happy to ring around the bike shops looking for a BT 020. I could have managed that bit but the convoluted replies that turned out to be promising the same thing except made by Pirelli or Michelin, would have been more taxing. In the end we find one in Aranda de Duero, 70 odd Km away and half way to Madrid. Oh well so that's the way I am going. I was wondering whether I would get to see my Madrid friends; now I can arrange to meet up with them at El Escorial. No, I am not going to ride into the middle of Madrid looking for their house. I did it once in my van with one of them to direct me and that was bad enough. I take it easy on the motorway direct to Aranda and the helpful V-Twin bike shop where my tyre change is made. Now back to the back roads, get into those little white ones... And swinging out of a village I quickly halt on the hard shoulder, fumbling to rip off the gloves, loosen helmet and off with the shades, scrabbling for the binoculars from around my neck... Yes! I can still see that flapping shape that is towing a rope. This Eagle has dangling and still squirming in its talons a snake at least a metre long and pretty thick. Another day I very nearly hit a brilliant green one of similar size (that really got the adrenalin going). The Eagle adjusts its grip a few times and as it heaves its way upward the snake's struggles cease. Short-toed Eagle I conclude, though if I was a snake catcher I'm sure I'd prefer to have long toes. In the bushes beside me a tiny Firecrest flits as the Eagle drifts from sight and I become aware of the heat now I am stationary.

On to the tight winding roads that scale the Sierra de la Guadarrama where the scent of pines has to be pushed through. Here one comes upon tall, striped poles that flank the road; they are perhaps 2.5 metres high; snow poles for the winter! On these roads if a warning sign says 30Km it is well to take it literally. It might be just sharp but on the other hand you may find yourself with a hairpin that without the drop would be a dual carriageway. I stop at the pass top, Puerta de Navafria (1773 metres), and watch a flock of Serin, and the occasional Crossbill. I become aware of a harsh rhythmically spaced call that reminds me of our Welsh Ravens, this though has a harder and even stronger note that reaches long across the vast emptiness that borders the ramparts of the Sierra. Looking for the source I see, soaring majestically, two Eagles and realise with great excitement that I am seeing Imperial Eagles for the first time. The Eagle of the Italian Airforce and thence Moto Guzzi was once common across the mountains of the Mediterranean, now it is restricted to protected fastnesses though gaining in recent years in strength and numbers. When the Eagle has drifted away a silence falls as I look out over the great plain stretching away into the heat haze. Then a faint disturbance, as if of a distant shore, a whisper of wind in pine needles that starting miles away grows and grows in such a rush that I find myself looking almost with trepidation for the oncoming tsunami of air getting louder and louder as it rushes towards me. Suddenly its breath is over me and deadwood clonks and branches fret as if they too are awed by its passing.

Coming down from the Puerta the road takes all my concentration, not just because I am still scrubbing in my new tyre but also because the obvious effects of the weather extremes have damaged the road surface and add to the dangers of twist and hairpin. Longitudinal cracks have been filled with tar, and in the heat become liquid snakes. These are seriously slippery and are quite frequently just where you want your line to be. In addition the odd bovine, or its spoor can be seen.

Once when I got off to take a picture and sit in the sun I gradually had the feeling I was being watched and eventually discerned a big black shape peering at me through the trees, somewhat unnerved a rather hasty mount-up ensued though I kept telling myself 'its just nosy'. Only one thing to do, just take it easy, slow right down. The plains will come up to meet one eventually. There is quite a contrast from the stillness and scented air high on the mountain to the busy roads and crowds of El Escorial. There is a definite feeling of the swirling skirts of the great city of Madrid that will one day probably reach all the way to these mountain slopes. Built by King Philip II to honour San Lorenzo (St. Lawrence) after a defeat of the French on the Saint's day in 1557 (August 10th). It is a fortress, monument, palace and monastery with one of the best stocked libraries in the world. It commands the town and its monumental structure is visible for many miles and covers an area of over 30,000 square meters. It has 9 towers, 9 organs, 16 patios, 73 statues, 86 sets of stairs, 88 fountains, 300 cells, 1,200 widows, more than 1,600 paintings and 2,673 doors. Very imposing, so clean in line and stark that it could have been built last year rather than over 400 centuries ago. I hunt down the 'Camping El Escorial'. Dreadful place, don't go! Expensive, unfriendly, dusty and you have to get a ticket from the machine on the wall in order to buy a cup of coffee. Early next day I am returning to El Escorial, where I shall meet my friends, when I see a bike outside a Hostal/Bar. I stop and find a great place to stay, not expensive, friendly and with a big garage for the bike. I take most of the luggage off the bike and then set out for the Valle de los Caidos - The Valley of the Lost Souls, Franco's monument to himself, thinly disguised as being for 'all the fallen' of that dreadful Civil War. A granite cross hundreds of feet high dominates a valley that cuts like an open wound into the side of the Sierra. The base of the cross is surrounded by monumental sculptures typical of the fascist, or for that matter, the soviet dictatorship. A soulless place indeed, no wonder many Spanish detest it. Though having sight-seen I spend a happy hour lying on a hillside listening to the wind in the pines and again the 'gahk - gahk' of the high Imperial Eagle. That evening I have a typical encounter with Spanish friends, one that moves from one mangled conversation topic to another, whilst we wander the streets and stop here and there for coffee, vino or tapas. The next morning I am headed back for Burgos but decide to fit in a quick visit to Segovia (as I have never been there). It is well worth the detour as the roman aqueduct dominating the town is very impressive. And on the way I have caught a glimpse of my elusive favourite; the Hoopoe.

I miss a turning leaving Segovia but take the next one which rewards me with a stretch of wooded riverine coolness full of bird song. Before I can get back to my intended route I cross sky-skimming stubble fields with Crested Larks for company. A 20km ruler-straight line of new tarmac (very tempting to the right hand) leads from Cuellar to Penafiel and another great castle crowning a rocky ridge above the town. In Roa where I stop to get some bread the town square by the church is packed. A popular wedding is on and those not in finery have come to see those that are. In another

back-road village I am surprised by a number of very well-painted murals on the side of buildings or in odd roadside alcoves. Another village happens to have a nice little picnic spot by a river with benches and a drinking fountain. I share the view of a very old stone bridge with Bonelli's Warbler and a flock of happy Crossbills. Cost of my lunch of bread, cheese and a glass of wine was hardly two euros. I eventually arrive back in Burgos having detoured again through the Sierra de la Demanda, another case of taking a very long way round that has been full of unforeseen and delightful experiences, including Booted and Bonelli's Eagles. A last paseo and visit to the old town. Next day: cross-country (of course) to Bilbao and the Whale-watching return ferry.

As the wall of the Cantabrians is left behind I have a bright idea! Next summer I will offer a week-long 'Five Eagles Tour'; a bird watching run on great roads and by many interesting places, combined with the Whale/Dolphin and seabird-watching on board the Bilbao ferry.

i) Soldiers who volunteered for the first assault on a breach would get promotion; if they survived, which as they would draw the defenders first fire and mines etc was not all that likely.

ii) They have been observed dropping bones from a height onto rocks to break them so they can get at that marrow.

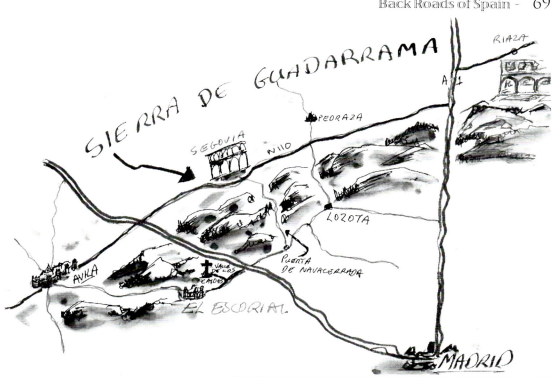

Salas de los Infantes

Segovia

SEÑORITA DORADITA MEETS DON DUNCAN

Doradita was quite enjoying retirement... Lazing around, no deadlines... No after school madness. But... But... There was a distinct lack of action! True she wasn't getting mauled by the 'niños' who used to try and feed her to the dog. Her patch of rubble had a sunny outlook and the vultures overhead gave an interesting pattern of silhouette and drifting shadow. Of course it was an advantage not being able to smell anything, as the air was somewhat tainted by the odour of the landfill site at the entrance of which she sat. Sometimes she imagined she was a Warden or Gatekeeper, clocking in the big lorries, though they only covered her with flying white dust from the gritty track. Then one day a new thunder came up the dirt track from the main road. A big V-Twin at low revs thumped its great heartbeat up to the gates.

A bright yellow motorcycle, that wasn't going to deliver much in the way of rubbish. The rider stopped and swiftly removed helmet and jacket and grabbed up a pair of binoculars and gazed through them at the sky. He seemed to be watching the circling birds with enjoyment. What a life, roaming the lands on that two wheeled-beast, always new and interesting things to experience. Suddenly retirement seemed stale, here was adventure! All those things she had missed seeing from inside that rubbish van. After a short time the bike thundered into life and left in a swirl of dust. Doradita was sad to see it go...

My recce three days before had proved this was still a great site for the big raptors. Now with four bikers behind me I was well pleased with the display. Hundreds of huge birds with wingspans 2 meters and more were drifting far up into the sky. Close by Griffon Vultures hunched like old men on the bare rocks of the hillside where the air temperature had to be in the high thirties °C, Red and Black Kites cruised

like null-gravity Lardy-Davidsons across the tip. A trio of White storks, strangely reminiscent of Peter Crouch, delicately stabbed at the bin bags, they had no doubts that they could pierce the feeble defences. Meanwhile James and Ian were trying to find some relief in releasing the steam from inside

their leathers; Charlie and Richard in their Gore-Tex were slightly better suited to Spanish riding but were still struggling with the high temperatures. I love the heat.

I did the Ornithological bit (forked tail, broad hand to the wing etc), after all this was the Biking and Birds trip. The numbers of great birds that slid across that hard, sharp blue sky was very impressive. I grabbed my camera and headed into the tip for a close up of a Griffon...

Doradita was excited at the re-appearance of the Moto Guzzi's fierce beat, now it was followed by the more mellow throb of three BMW's and as a tail end Charlie, the civilised sound of a VFR750 Honda. If only, if only she could some how hitch a ride. Luckily her thumb was stuck up all ready, cos' that was how her solid plastic hands were cast. Trouble was how to get one of those riders to notice her. She tried her loudest possible thought, straining out 'Hola, caballero! Aqui!'. For a long moment nothing happened, the riders removed kit and watched the first rider wander off into the tip with his camera. Then one of them laughed and a big hand reached down, and before she could think 'Gracias', she was safely snugged in behind the cargo net on the back of the yellow Centauro.

It nearly didn't happen; the Five Eagles tour. In mid-May one of my trio of 'clients' had to have a major operation and would not be able to take part, his friend also dropped out, leaving just Charlie. Luckily he had a friend, who despite just having returned from a continental bike trip, was willing to have another. Then on the way to the Plymouth ferry his BMW developed a fault and he missed the ferry. Not to be deterred (the hero) Richard got the bike fixed and caught a ferry to Roscoff. 700 miles or so later he caught up with us the evening of Charlie's arrival in Spain. Meanwhile Charlie got talking to two BMW riders on the Ferry, the upshot of which was that James and Ian tagged along on the tour for the first two days to Jaca.

Now weeks after the end of the trip my scribbled notes seem so dry and minimal. It is quite hard to imagine that it happened and that it was such a great immersion in riding, Spain and the camaraderie of the road. But as I concentrate on trying to picture the noted moment, the memories drift up to be tasted like many different tapas, sharp and tangy, hot and cold, seafood, meat and sweet pimentoes.

The techno-marvel of mobile phones and, yes, the GPS came into play in Santander. I had arrived in Spain two days early (Portsmouth to Bilbao). I had arranged to meet Charlie at the petrol station on the edge of the park where the ferry disgorges itself: Except it didn't because the whole road system along the front is being re-made and disembarkation traffic exits somewhere that I never found (through the docks). I had one of those interesting discussions with a Spaniard whilst stopped at the roadside trying to spot the exit point. He liked the bike;, he was a somewhat camp retired merchant seaman and liked to practise his English, whilst I practised my Spanish – but he couldn't tell me where the ferry traffic would appear. I headed out of town and found the first lay-by on the N623. I started trying call Charlie's mobile. Eventually I got him and heard the news of the missing Richard. It took a couple of hours to finally meet and this was down to the fact that James's GPS was able to steer them from the wrong road out of Santander to the right one on which I waited. Away we went. It was a new experience having to ride with the constant attention to those following as well as to the traffic and the birds. I pulled us in to a great little place to stop for food 2Km after Puente Viesgo (28Km out of Santander). Meson St Domingo has a bar, restaurant and Motel. Here we were treated to a fantastic tortilla (omelette) bocadillos, a beer and water. Refreshed we swung up the great Cantabrian mountain wall, the group settling in and the views opening up. We didn't take the

direct road to Burgos but turned off at the great Embalse de Ebro onto the lesser N232. Later we took to the white roads for the first sightseeing stop at the castle perch of Poza de la Sal. The hewn steps leading up to the castle entrance are worn by endless feet over hundreds of years; they are slippery and deeply rounded. It would have been a hard job to attack up this, and UK Health and Safety would have a fit at the general public being asked to use them. Standing on the top of Poza de la Sal the Castle sits narrowly on its mighty rock spine. One could spit down the chimneys of the town three hundred feet below, if one had spit to spare in the dry heat and after climbing those narrow steep steps.

Cross-country we ride the tiny roads that are mostly traffic-clear, sometimes pristine tarmac, sometimes a washboard that has to be taken slow, or fast enough to smooth out the teeth loosening effect. Wide open wheat fields lead to a hidden cleft that drops one into pine trees and then a baking hillside from which the wild herbs swipe at the nose. Another little pueblo with a bar for refreshing beer and water in the cool

interior. Finally we arrive at the excellent Hostal Acanto and ride down into the cool depths of their underground car park. Michelin route return trip Burgos to Santander is 220 miles; I have clocked up 360, this is typical of the extra miles I manage to fit in to each day's journey.

Second day and the fanciful crenellated castle at Olite, tapas including a not much appreciated callos that was rather too much like sludgy innards (which is what it was). A superb bikers' dream of a road that sweeps side to side with hardly a straight, and clean crisp tarmac. This a 'hoon' road and I have given the lads a rendezvous at the other end so that we can all enjoy it at our own pace. As we leave the town the Guzzi howls into life as I wind it full on and climb the needle over the ton. For a little while the dancing fireflys of the BMWs of James and Ian diminish in my mirrors, then they start creeping back. When they get close I wave them past. I can't enjoy the road with one eye in the mirror... The big RT slides past with a silk-ripping swish, the GS close behind. I go back to enjoying the view as well as the road. As we close with the Pyrenees the distant jagged peaks rear up shouldered by snow. The weeks before our arrival had seen quite a lot of un-seasonal rain to our benefit as the wild flowers were strong and bright across the canvas of the land. We stop by an ancient ivy curtained bridge, I reckon it is hot enough for a dip and climb into the river. My breath is dragged forth by the cold and gasping I climb hurriedly back out.

As the list of Eagles reaches the fifth with a Short-toed, (Golden, Imperial, Bonelli's and Booted already spotted), Charlie adds another, the Blonde Topped Eagle, found fairly frequently to our delight, generally in bars and hotels! Having glided down from the high Navafria pass (1773 mts) over the Sierra Guadarrama a very nice Rumanian one chats to us as we try to avoid the conversation of a drunken Moroccan who wants to get in on the conversation. It was 24 degrees at the 'cool' pine-clad top, 35 degrees 20 minutes later; which necessitated the beer and water stop. In the Guadarrama I became afflicted with the curse of 'grip-fear'! Due to heavy winter snows (the Sierra tops out at over 6,000') the roads crack apart, and are repaired with tar that in the summer heat become semi-liquid snakes. After a relatively small 'sideways-slideyway and twitch' I find myself slowing drastically into every corner. It takes many miles and a conscious effort to push back to normal confidence.

Azure-winged Magpie's flit and squawk in the brush where we look down into the cool cañon of the Rio Lobos. We are riding under one of those big skies that partner the huge flat plains of wheat, pushing at a hard cross-wind that is un-fettered by the distant mountains. I try a new route that seems to follow a river and does have some trees and low buffs to give some respite. Now suddenly I can smell distant rain, though here the heat stills beats down, and up, from the hot tarmac and dusty roadsides. The wind strengthens and seems to carry a threat of thunder. At the next small town (Cuellar) we find a shuttered Hotel on an empty

square. I push the intercom and eventually get a woman's voice. At first she is reluctant to appear or give us rooms but bad Spanish and persistence is rewarded by lovely en-suite hugely timbered, high-ceilinged rooms. There is no parking except the street outside, but my geranium-hung balcony is right above. That night the long-threatened storm breaks with massive flashes of lightning and claps of thunder that are almost drowned out by the roar of the pelting rain. In the morning everything including the bikes is beautifully washed clean. The sun is back in a clear blue sky and as we ride we suck up the sparkling fresh, after-rain air.

Stopping outside the medieval walls of Burgo El Osma we burrow through a street market where I top up my wardrobe with trousers and three pairs of socks for 10 euros. Crossing the river on an old stone bridge we have to dodge a fisherman's flying hook. We enter a Plaza Mayor in front of a grand church, getting beers we sit and watch a huge and very well-dressed wedding party gradually exit the church and cross the square for the reception. A tension builds, photographer lurks,

we join everyone else in mounting anticipation. At last the glorious bride comes out, dodging a rain of rice and serenaded by a singer and guitars.

Charlie and Richard are both pilots (Helicopters to Jumbos) and it was interesting how quickly they caught on to the spotting and identification of distant soaring Eagles and Vultures. They were probably at least as quick as myself and I stopped pointing out all but the most spectacular or unusual birds. They also seemed pretty damn quick at spotting the Blonde Topped Eagles!

It was interesting that all the bikes (V10 Moto Guzzi, BMW R1200GS, R1200RT and Honda VFR750) coped with the varied terrain. Though they could be graded on the dirt and hardcore section we encountered on the Najera road (which by next year could be one of the 'great rides' in its new tarmac coat); from the GS's, V10, RT down to the VFR that was a little less happy. Of course on the 'hoon' sections the RT and VFR led the field.

I learnt a lot about leading a group of riders, as I have very rarely travelled in a group. I think for James and Ian whose normal biking was a track day or long, fast blasts between target locations (fuelled by the use of GPS?), the cross-country concentration and wrestling was harder work than they expected. It was great to share different outlooks and pleasures gained from the views, humour and experience of the others. Perhaps 200 miles is a comfortable daily maximum for a mixed group. Other riders may need more breaks than I take on my own, and more frequently at bars rather than picnicking out in the wilds as I often do.

MAIN BIRD LIST: Eagles - Golden, Imperial, Bonelli's, Booted, Short-toed. Vultures - Griffon, Black, Egyptian. Goshawk, Sparrowhawk, Peregrine, Kestrel. Red Kite, Black Kite. Buzzard. Hoopoe, Wallcreeper, Blue Rock Thrush, White Stork, Crested Lark, Night Heron, Little Egret, Black Redstart, Bee-eater.

Swallowtail Butterfly

Griffon Vulture

Riglos

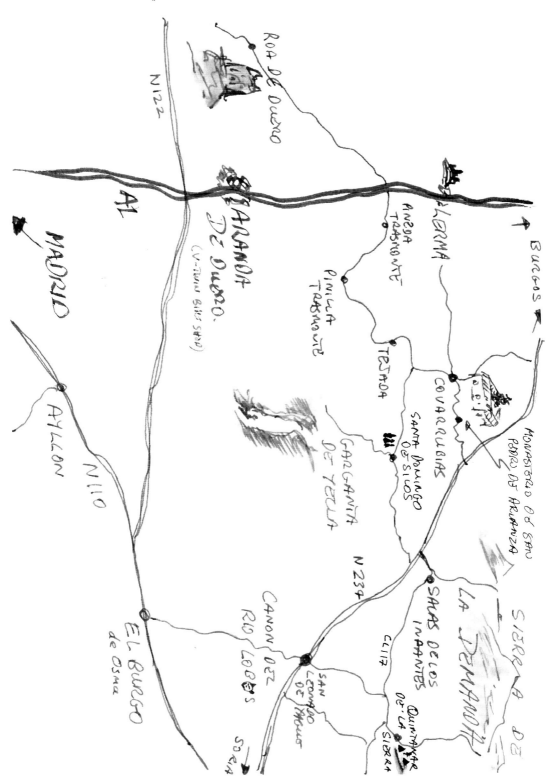

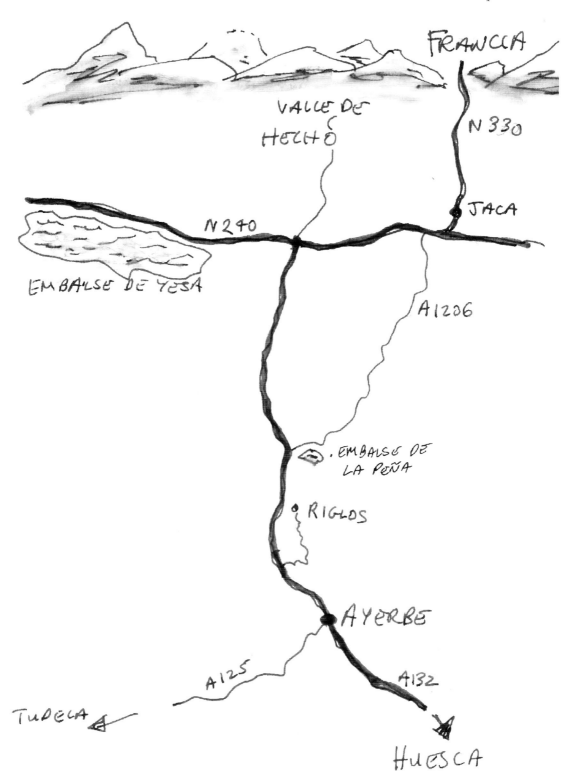

The Beckoning Horizon.

For some of us there is always a beckoning horizon. How ever much one can try to live without looking up, concentrating on the day to day pleasures and work of family and business, you catch yourself gazing at the line between sky and land, and errant thoughts slip in that if allowed to, coalesce saying – 'I want to split that line and find the next, push outward and onward.'

I NEED TO TRAVEL! The biggest part of that is the going. Yes, I prefer to go to Spain, that is because my travelling is rationed. If I could go many places in a year I would go wherever a ticket took me – including the moon (and I really mean that).

Travelling alone is actually very different from travelling with someone or some-many. Not that compromise is a minus but it means the way you travel, stop, stay, eat and sleep is defined by a combined entity – you and... Travel on your own and the bad decisions as well as the good ones are all down to YOU. No excuses, you got it wrong or you got it right, or close enough. Here if you push yourself further than you should, make bad decisions or drop the bike in the stupidest of ways it is only you the witness and only you the victim. Both travellings are equally valid and equally rewarding.

How many times when you are on your own do you hit a perfect curving road with awesome views and a Golden Eagle in a tree watching you perfect the apex... And there is no-one there to share it with. Except yourself of course, but it would be nice to be able to stop down the mountain and say "wasn't that great"... Share the

joy, share the experience. Thing is you might not have ridden that road unless you were on your own. In our quantum universe there are so many realities and the one you took because you were on your own was then the one you experienced which was different from the one you travelled with 'A. N. Other'. At the end of September I was again in Spain, on this day I changed my mind and direction at least five times.

Leaving Burgos I first think to go west for a change but get confused round the new ring road and end up heading East. Oh well, I'll head for the campsite at Quintanar de la Sierra instead. But as I turn off the Camino de Santiago (N120) towards Arlanzon I get a very strong smell of rain ahead and the Sierra de la Demanda where I am headed is shrouded in dark dank cloud. I decide to turn around and think to go south-east towards Soria though within a few miles I see that the sun is only to the south. Oh well, let's head south then. Let's go to Segovia. On the map there is a campsite between there and Avila. I blast it down the Madrid motorway to the gates of the Guadarrama where I turn off for Segovia. Arriving I park up opposite the roman aqueduct (by the big roundabout you can go up onto the pavement and park) and stop for a coffee. It is early yet so

I decide to go onto a campsite supposedly near the Embalse las Gogetas at Avila, I get there after much going round in circles trying to get off the A51 outer bypass and attempts to find the Valladolid road off which I expect the campsite. Eventually I get to the Embalse but there are no signs of a campsite. So I look for more campsites on the map and decide to head for one at Burgohondo on the AV-900 (a great road by the way) which cuts off from the N403 Toledo road as you are leaving Avila. I arrive and there are no signs for a campsite, only a dim pump attendant who says that the road towards another possible one at Navaluenga is 'cortado for obras' and he doesn't know of any other... So map-looking seems to be a choice of more unknowns or to head right over the Sierra de Gredos to Casavieja where I have camped before and so know it exists. What a ride! I up the pace and am pushing on as the sun is lowering and the sky turning tangerine in long streaks of alto cirrus. The Gredos mountains loom massively ahead and the road is a constant switch back as it climbs the 1000 feet to the Puerta de Mijares (around 5,000' above sea level). Then the same again all the way down. Always a huge drop off, sometimes the road ahead is so close under the one you are on you can't see it at all. I get into the campsite as dusk falls. The reception is shut but the barriers are open so I go and set up my tent at warp speed as it is rapidly getting dark. With the tent up and my sleeping bag shaken out I can at last heat up my tin of cocido madrilène (chickpeas in a mild spicy sauce with bits of chorizo and pork), which is very good with the remains of my bread and washed down with a carton of rough red wine. Finally a mug of coffee as the wind in the pines and the scent of the mountain in the warm darkness closes around me. It is very quiet, there seems to be no one else on the site. Cicadas and crickets the only orchestra as the stars gleam down. A tawny owl calls... I call back and he replies a little worried at this intruder. Around 350 km for the day. Next morning I start typing this seated in the sun on a warm rock, only the sound of the rushing little stream and occasionally the wind in the pines, the scent of which is subtly growing as the sun warms them. Suddenly I am bombarded by swearing and bits of pine cone. Looking up I find an enormous Red Squirrel in the top of the tree I am leaning against. As the mountains are twice the size of UK ones so are the squirrels!

In July 07 waiting to board the ferry out I had got talking to a biker from Bristol.

We quickly discovered many similar interests; carpentry, design, ecology. Nick decided to travel to Burgos with me the first day before heading on to Madrid where he was meeting a girl. I started by taking him to see the castle at Poza but via the Puerta de la Mazorra which unfortunately has recently been remade; the hairpins bent outward and cambered; just doesn't have the thrill it used to have. Seeking some new roads we go to Frias and discover a great little castled town. With other wanderings we take 7 hours to do the 100 odd miles from Santander to Burgos. Part of this is stopping more frequently, taking more time and discussion over a beer or a coffee, accommodating things the other wants to look at. A good example being the next day when I would have ridden past the dead-end road that leads to the Santuario de Santa Casilda but Nick wanted to see the church. He was right, it was well worth it. Before we parted south of Jadraque we visited the medieval town, of Ayllon and crossed the Sierra del Pela ending up on 15 kms of dirt track which was kind of interesting! It was a somewhat hairy ride with deep sand or small marble-like stones. It was good to know that if one came off or had a puncture there was someone on hand to help. We made it through okay (Fazer and Centauro)

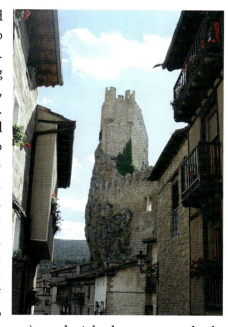

and picked up a great little road to Jadraque where the interesting castle was unfortunately under repair and shut. I headed for Cuenca and found more great back roads. We met again in Albacete where with the help of another girlfriend of Nick's I got my broken brake pedal fixed for 20 euros. Travelling on we parted just before Toledo and met again in Avila. A trip enhanced by a chance friendship.

This year I cut through the Sierra de la Pena de Francia travelling from the Talavera battlefield to Ciudad Rodrigo, another Peninsular War site, and one that I would definitely fit into my 'Battlefields of the Peninsular War' bike tour. What a road! The tarmac better than in the Sierra Guadarrama where the winter cracks are filled with slimy liquid tar in the summer. The sweeping bends are a clean joy

Sanctuario de St Casilda. Un Vultures.

that sends a fizz of delight through one, tempting greater through speed... Until, like a boa constrictor they begin to tighten and tighten again. Soon you are unable to see where the road goes for its route barely peeps through the curtains of the languorous pine trees that put the fresh into air. From gaily swinging into the corner in third one is reduced to dropping it to second or first in case you find yourself going back up your own tailpipe. Finding a dirt run-off on such a corner I am going slowly enough to take the bike off the road and park up. Quickly stripping off my jacket I bathe in the scent and heat of the mountainside. As the bike ticks its heat away I get out my piece of

sausage, cheese and bread and the water bottle. I travel for days with these staples as my lunch and sometimes supper and find my stomach shrinks its appetite and my mind finds as much enjoyment as in a full restaurant meal. For half an hour I lie under the pines eating, relaxing and listening to the rhythmic rise and fall of engines, lorries or cars and the occasional bike that are negotiating this road. Rested I continue and eventually come out on the main road into Ciudad. I see a lot of bikes and then signs MOTO with an arrow. I vaguely follow them as they go towards the castle walls I want to see. I get there and find there is a massive 'Concentracion de Moto' a bike rally. I wonder whether to sign up and stay... But I am not that interested in the advertised Lesbian striptease and the pointless maxing of poor little pseudo race bikes (that pop and bang scaring the passersby) decides me. I shall re-mount and head onward. Under the stretching sky lie sun-baked pueblos, pine scented mountains; a land of as yet hidden experiences waiting only for my arrival...

Later I am sitting on the balcony of my room in Hotel Juan II - Toro, a glass of local (bought in the town) a 'joven', young and fresh, but well rounded, drinking from my ceramic Brittany Ferries yoghurt pot. I am nibbling at bread left over from my picnic by a canal where I had the joyful, brilliant azure flash of a Kingfisher. Right down there is the Duero and the old bridge into Toro. There is a causeway/race at the bridge and fisherman stand on its shallow flow whilst the rush and roar of the tumult of the slipway comes up to me in a constant sound that is only varied in tempo by the vagrant breeze. The dark pointing fingers of cypresses line the path that goes from the plaza to my right (where the church stands) down to the end of the bridge a hundred feet or more below me. Beyond the river stretches a panorama of fields in various shades of green that rise, a gentle quilt to low hills on the horizon. The sky is enormous in its blueness. If my view is a circle then the whole top half of that circle is sky... In the barrio to my right children are playing, their cries fly up as swift as the pigeons returning to the cathedral's crannies and cliffs. What is special about these days is this, I am selfishly but also experientially alone, no agreed time to do anything, no targets other than mine own which I try to leave as much to whim as possible. The peace floods into my very soul. Part of being here is that I can be as sociable or unsociable as I like. If

I want to engage, understand and initiate conversation I can, if not I can let all the sounds of language drift past me.

The journey of life is a singular one, however close you stand to others. In reality the wide screen of every experience is yours alone, even half an hour later your and their descriptions of the same event will be different. Too often we reach for the camera; not all experiences should be 'parked up' in memory; some, like a passing scent, should be left as faint watermarks upon our unconscious, the effect that of the moment, not hardened into a frame by time and date. As a child we relish experience as much as the result. "Do it again! Again! And again!" Our adult mind gets annoyed, "You've done that. Try this". We have missed the point, the child is not doing it in order to be able to say "I've done that", they are enjoying the experience purely for it's pleasure, and so are more than happy to repeat it. It is too easy to put events into the photo album of our lives to be brought out for special occasions. "There. I did that!" I say let every experience change you. Don't let the adult in you limit your memories to the material events you have parked in the multi-storey of your outer lives.

Don't let awareness be bludgeoned by second-hand experience that saves us any real pain or discomfort by being filtered through other's eyes.

Like Don Quixote, set forth with your imagination and little else...

Robert Louis Stevenson said it:

"I travel not to go anywhere, but to go."

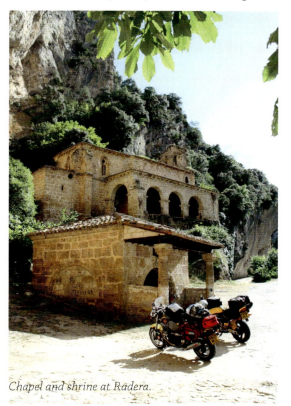

Chapel and shrine at Radera.

The very helpful boss of the motorbike shop in Albacete who fixed my broken brake pedal by plating it together, for €20.

Part of my sketchbook -
Zamora, the Plaza Mayor
church and Pedraza castle -
from a convenient bar!

Plaza Mayor - Zamora

Castillo de Pedraza

Modern castle at Bargas.

The *walls of Avila with swirling, screaming Swifts.*

Edge

Where is your edge? How far do you go? What happens if you lose your edge?
There are the edges which define an entity and there are the edges that give an advantage.
The edge of skill and the edge of experience, the edge of life and the edge of self, these are
closely woven together. I believe we select band, of men and women that ride motorbikes,
generally know a bit more about edges than the commonality. The Skill edge is the
real, or imagined to be real, limit of your own bravery; in life and in the riding of your
motorbike. It seems to me that most humans instinctively make every effort to surround
themselves with boundary cushions. Of course this is the basis of 'society'. Though there
are free spirits that, like the mountain men of the Old West are always in search of a new
horizon; but most of us happily settle into a rigidity. A set way of riding, a set of roads,
a set of club friends. After a while you don't push your skills any more, don't try and get
round that corner smoother, we are comfortable, and it is easier to stick with what we
know. Now and again, sometimes by accident, we suddenly reach or cross that edge. A
miscalculation or an unforeseen tractor causes us to push our skill to a new edge, or back
out to where it used to be. Other times, particularly with our fraternity, the Mountain
Man inside will break out; we pack light and head for the mountains of a new land. We
step over the edge of day to day experience and challenge our own skills with the risk of
the unknown and unforeseeable. Soon the comfort zone of experience is expanded, we
cope with things that previously the mere thought of would have scared us. I know that
times when I haven't been riding for a week or more I set out in a cautious way. I worry
whether it is going to rain, how far my petrol will take me and so which petrol station
am I going to stop at. Ooh, is the road slippery or is something wrong with my tyres, did
the engine always sound as rattly as that? Ted Simon describes this very well in Jupiter's
Travels - "my ear picked up noises and vibrations that fed my doubts. - I was unwilling to
believe that all this proceeded from my own mind, and I tried to diagnose faults. - looked

at the wheel alignment and several times snatched a glance at my rear tyre, convinced it must be flat." This happened after a rest period in Kenya. He had pushed his edges well out getting there but it is instructive to see how quickly they had contracted around him as he rested up and 're-civilised' himself. Coming back from even a relatively short bike trip I am relaxed, taking the road and weather as it comes. Petrol, well, I have 30-40 miles from the reserve light coming on, plenty of time. The edges of riding skill and the travel challenges we are willing to tackle surround our sense of self. When you ride well and far, you can reach for that point of existence in which you are responding to the world as it comes to meet you, freed of the desire to know everything in advance and to impose your will upon it in advance. Able to go with the flow. Comfortable with a new expanded outer edge.

A honed knowledge of our skill edge allows us to better handle the edges of experience. As in 'The Outlaw Josey Wales'. "The Western outlaw usually faced high odds. Beyond their physical, practised dexterity with the pistol and their courage, those who "done the thinkin'" were the ones who lasted longest. They always endeavoured an "edge". - To his reckless men Bloody Bill Anderson had been a master tutor of the "edge". Once he told Josey, "Iff'n I'm to face out and outlast another feller in the hot sun... all I want is a broom straw to hold over my head fer shade A little edge and I'll beat'em." He knew the limits of his skill so well that all he needed was the extra advantage given by a piece of straw. This edge is the one that lets you safely expand. You don't have to spit gobs of tobacco juice onto a dogs head to make it work for you. Draw from beyond your own skill; this is the use of world that is rushing at you to tilt the odds in your favour. Whether getting the sun in your opponent's eyes or knowing that the big lorry that has been going just too fast to be comfortably overtaken is now going to be slow coming out of that next corner. Be ready; you might well have the edge now to nip past. Like Josey's knife sharp edge of action, being close to your edge is to be able to react with purpose and decision. We bikers often meet it like Josey meeting Ten Bears, the Comanche Chief; alone. Josey sets the edge of his skill before Ten Bears, ("this is the word of life, and of death...") and Ten Bears sees the truth of this edge. They become blood brothers with the pain of a knife cut across the palm because Ten Bears sees that Josey Wales is poised at the very edge of his existence. Josey knows a wrong move and he will instantly be killed and yet Ten Bears can see that Josey is in equilibrium, perfectly balanced, able to go for death or life with equal commitment. And that is his true edge, his best advantage, the knowledge of self edge. This is an edge rooted in attitude born out of aptitude. The result of the sharpening of the self edge is the ways in which we respond to others and the world around us. Our sense of self-sufficiency fostered by the testing of our edge on two wheels enhances our ability to cope with the hard edges of experience that come at us. We bikers are 'individualists' - acknowledged fact. One reason is because edges define personality and we spend more time at our edges and keep them sharper than the hoi-paloi.

I am not saying that we should always be trying to push out the edges, but that we should occasionally check that we haven't let them drift closer and become a fuzzy band of 'can't be bothered'.

So... Breath deep, fill your lungs, push out the chest of your life, discard that suit and head for them thar hills!

I have just finished the short, sharp reading of A. L. Kennedy's 'On Bullfighting'. A book that has the same vicarious and voyeuristic fascination as the thought of watching the corrida does.

It is an enticing read which was over all too quick but it resonated for me in a number of ways.

Here, in the telling of her search for the meaning of life and death in, and out of the bullring, there is caught, as in

Biking and Bullfighting

a muddy reflection, the truth of many a bike ride and rider. Look: The matador is a man (and fewer women) set somewhat apart from the saner whole of humanity. Those who would not dream of playing with death in such an obvious way. For them it is sufficient to overeat, take noxious substances and drive badly in the false safety of metal boxes. The biker however knows that death and injury are very real risks every time he goes out and faces the unpredictable savagery of the roads.   The matador goes through a ritual to dress himself for the event: The tights, the waistcoat and the special shoes through to the stiff and heavy, instant identifier of the chaquetilla, the short jacket. Finally the montera the thick felt hat. The parallels in the ritual one undergoes most times one rides are self-evident. The biker though is generally less aware of what he is beginning. He does not have the portable altar of religion and 'lucky' mascots that the matador touches before he leaves his hotel room to walk to his appointment. Though some of us have our little hidden away superstitions; an order of enrobing, cleaning visor or goggles, or a lucky rabbits-foot on the key ring. Each encased in the armour of our activity we go forth with a heightened pulse. Kennedy does an excellent job of bringing us to the matador's side. I see the same experience being enacted by the biker. We face dangers that we can generally see coming, and as with the matador we believe that we have the skill to defeat them. And like the matador we are sometimes mistaken: Despite all our best efforts to stack the odds in our favour we can be gored or killed by the unexpected or the unforeseen. That is precisely why we do it. Particularly in our, so-protectionist state where even if you hunger for the respite of death to release you from terminal pain and disease you will be pilloried or prosecuted. Ride your bike and face the snorting-black, hook-horned death and when you return to the safe world and the last echoes of olé and exhaust howl have died away, then you know you are alive. Once again you have found definition; an edge, to your existence. Carlos Castaneda's Don Juan talked of becoming aware of one's death as a shadow, always just behind your shoulder - always moments away from touching you on that shoulder and summoning you to cross the divide. You must not become mesmerised by the shadow, running from it (because you can't), or live a plan-less life in fear of it. But through acknowledgement of its presence you can achieve a higher sense of being. Live life to the full because that shadow is with you. Bikers and bullfighters; we both do that. Here is 'duende'. That sense-shifting Spanish word that appears in Flamenco and La Jota as well as the corrida. The spirit of life-force itself that transforms the practitioner, purifying as it sings through blood and brain. The dancer becomes the dance, the singer the song, and the matador and bull become interlaced in the dance of death.

Hidden within our helmets and essentially alone we do not often recognise it for what it is. But think back to a perfect series of overtakes, each one placing you right for the next, magically always at the right opening of road or gap in oncoming traffic. Suddenly you are not 'thinking' it through but melding with the world and the bike to slice effortlessly past death. Watch Foggy or any other great racer and there are times when you can see them come 'on song' as the 'duende' flows through them. This is only possible because of the blood on the sand that could be theirs or yours.

Riding or driving in Spain...

Remember to take spare lamps and a fluorescent vest, spare set of glasses if you wear them (required by law), and I have heard of people being fined for running out of petrol if they cause an obstruction.

Radar controlled Traffic Lights:
These are common but a little bit sneaky... You will see a big sign...

It says "too much speed and you get a stop light"... or similar. These first overheads are alternating flashing amber to tell you there is a radar. The next set will go RED if you or the vehicle in front or behind are exceeding the speed limit. The law says YOU MUST STOP for the RED... If you do it will almost instantaneously go back to amber flashing, which means 'keep going with care'. Many (perhaps most) spanish drivers do not actually stop at the RED, they just go straight through, so if you have come to a halt you may get tailgated. Therefore, a) watch your rear, b) check just in case there is a pedestrian crossing or side road coming in to add to the mix, c) if in doubt pull over and pretend to check your map whilst watching what everyone else is doing!

You will generally realise very quickly that some of your habits and instincts are now incorrect, but minor road junctions and roundabouts can still catch you out, fine when there is other traffic to remind you but not so easy when the road is empty and you rely on instinct: Come on a single track or un-demarcated road to a 'Give Way' junction with a main road and (if there is no traffic to warn you), it is all too easy to look the wrong way and pull out onto the wrong carriageway. Being aware of this propensity I always take a moment to think the road position through.   In the early years I used to have a little diagram stuck in my tank bag as a prompt for this and the right way to go round roundabouts.

If you see a series of stripes on the road surface they indicate a mild to severe dip in the road - speeding cars are leaving rubber as they reconnect with road.

Bends on back roads and others can be badly deformed around corners where big lorries have pushed up a fold in hot tarmac.

Road camber even on new looking roads can be wrong where they shouldn't be.
In the Guadarrama in particular, repairs to frost cracks can leave slimy tar snakes in the hot months.

If you see a sign saying "MAL ESTADO" it probably means it, probably a km later when you have stopped believing it, and right around a corner to something like this photo!

In the afternoon (2pm - 4pm) the roads are often almost completely deserted, tempting one to cut corners, off-side etc. Beware the odd Spanish driver will be doing the same, expecting no-one to be on the road, as they aren't most of the year.

You rarely see Police or Guadia Civil in the countryside, however it IS worth observing speed limits through little hamlets, particularly if there is a handy bar at lunch time. Generally speaking they are far more easy going and less rule-bound than ours; until you overstep the mark badly or obviously and then they will come down on you hard with a spot fine at the least.

DIY Spanish tapas evening...

Here is my little tapas kit; the wine jug picked up in a spanish market for very little (it's kind of magic because even cheapo wine seems to taste better out of it). The ceramic beakers are Brittany ferries yoghurt pots! They are great to drink out of and free (after you have enjoyed the yoghurt!) The small ceramic dishes I have found here and in Spain, I do also use some small Le Creuset lidded pots. These are the things you dump in them and then stick in a hot oven (around 150-190) for 20 mins or so, protect them with a foil top, you can take it off right at the end to brown the tops. All the following go in with olive oil (cold-pressed virgin preferably) and chopped garlic.

Chorizo - cut chunks off a sausage, about 15mm (1/2"+) thick.

Sliced mushrooms.

Prawns - the biggest you can afford with a dusting of paprika (oak smoked if possible).

If you have 'lean machine' or a heavy grill pan, get it hot and do thin sections of aubergine and courgette so they show the black stripes, then put them into a shallow dish, on with the oil and garlic. In the oven for 5 mins (if you have time and space), otherwise allow to cool.

If your guests are not the squeamish type then treating some squid the same way is a very Spanish addition.

Peppers, start these a little earlier. A red, green, yellow pack goes along way... slice so that the sections are fairly flat, put on foil under a hot grill, first do the inside till it softens, then turn over and do the skin side till it blisters, pull out and grabbing the skin (try not to burn yourself) pull it off. Slice and put in dish (the pepper not the skin) with a drizzle of oil over the top.

Crispy baguettes and a selection of your favourite cheeses.

An Ensilada Mixta - mixed salad, to be proper; tinned tuna on the top.

Make a tortilla (Spanish not Mexican), this can be served hot or cold. In spain you often get it as a filling for a bocadillo or baguette.

Peel and halve a few potatoes then boil or microwave them till they are pretty much cooked but still hold together. Fry fairly finely chopped onion and garlic until browned then chop the potatoes up into small pieces (watch out they will be hot) and give them a bit of a fry. How big a frying pan you have for the tortilla will determine the number of eggs required. The pan I use (above) is 290mm (11.5") across and I'll use at least 8 eggs and up to a dozen. Beat them up in a jug with some thyme and pepper, if you look short on eggs you can bulk it with a little bit of milk. I get the oil just smoking then pour enough egg in to cover the bottom, then distribute the potatoes, onion and garlic on top, then the rest of the eggs. On a reasonable heat within 5 to 10 mins you should be able to gently spatula up the edges and see the underside browning and firm. I now put the whole pan under a pre-heated grill to cook and brown the top. Alternatively you have to turn it over by putting a big plate on top, turn over then slide the the tortilla back into the pan, but this can be a risky business! Hot or cold slice, into wedges. Trial and error, as with all recipes, will let you fine tune the amounts, times, seasoning that suits you and your cooker. If the tortilla doesn't hang together like a cake when done then the following may apply: too much pots etc, not enough eggs, not cooked quick enough at the beginning.

A cheating Paella goes like this; fine chop the following ingredients: Chicken breast, onion, garlic, some peppers, a mushroom perhaps or a bit of courgette. Rinse Basmati rice well with cold water (one tea cup for two people), dump into boiling water with a teaspoon of tumeric in it, cook till just softening (5-10 mins). Meanwhile fry onion, peppers and garlic with some smoked paprika, once softening add the chicken and brown it, then the other veg. By now the rice is ready; rinse quickly with boiling water and add to the pan. Chuck in some frozen (or fresh) prawns and peas, pour over about a half pint of hot chicken stock and simmer till the rice is cooked and the peas and prawns are done. A good addition is to soak some saffron in oil for a while beforehand to add to the cooking or use one of the paella spice packs you can buy in any supermarket in Spain. I use that same pan (above) but you can do it in a wok just as easily.

Books, Websites etc.

The Adventures of Don Duncan;

        The Factory of Light by Michael Jacobs. ISBN 0-7195-6173-6

        Spanish Steps by Tim Moore. ISBN 0-224-06265-4

        Don Quixote by Miguel Cervantes. ISBN 0-436-20515-7

EDGE;

        'Jupiter's Travels' by Ted Simon. ISBN 0 14 00.5410 3

        'The Outlaw Josey Wales' (formerly 'Gone to Texas') by Forrest Carter. ISBN 0 8600 7331

9

Biking and Bullfighting;

        On Bullfighting by A.L.Kennedy ISBN 0-224-06099-6 Yellow Jersey Press (Randomhouse)

        The Teachings of Don Juan (and others) by Carlos Castaneda. ISBN 0-14-019238-7

        Duende by Jason Webster. ISBN 0-385-60361-4

Gerald Brennan books, all good reads:

        South from Granada. ISBN 0-14-016700-5

        The Spanish Labyrinth. ISBN 0-521-39827-4

And others.

        Roads to Santiago by Cees Nooteboom. ISBN 1-86046-419-X

        Ghosts of Spain by Giles Tremlett. ISBN 0-571-22167-X

        A Stranger in Spain by H.V. Morton. My copy is pre ISBN

        A great piece of fiction, one of the best books I've read in a long time - The Shadow of the
            Wind by Carlos Ruiz Zafón.

        Cathedral of the Sea by Ildefonso Falcones. ISBN 978-0-385-61185-5

        The Basque History of the World by Mark Kurlansky. ISBN 0-099-28413-8

        The Forging of a Rebel by Arturo Barea.

        Birds of Europe by Lars Jonsson. ISBN 0-7136-4422-2

        Watch the film 'Pan's Labyrinth' it is fantastic.

Michelin maps,

Motorcycle shops. V-Twin Motocycletas, Aranda de Duero Avda Castilla, 86 - Tel 947 512 748

Moto Margar, Calle La Roda, 25, Albacete . 967 672 000   www.motomargar.es

Hospederia del Desierto - Tabernas   www.hospederiadeldesierto.com

The Hospederia is 3* at the same place is the 2* Hostal Calatrava which is good value.

Hostal Acanto - Burgos   www.hostalacanto.com

Hostal Acuuarela - Burgos (new, closer into town, bike friendly) www.hostalacuarela.com

Hostal Boira - Jaca

El Rincon Castellano - Cuellar Hotel and Restaurant   www.elrinconcastellano.com

Hotel Avenida - Yecla Tel: 968 751 215 San Pascual,3,

Paradors - National   www.parador.es

Brittany Ferries - www.brittanyferries.com

P&O - www.poportsmouth.com

Both ferry companies are now pretty good about tying down motorbikes safely.

Vocabulario.

Best to get yourself a phrase book, I like an old BBC Spanish one I have had for years. Cassell's Colloquial Spanish (ISBN 0-304-07943-X) is a good read for pitfalls. You quickly learn that just by changing the pronunciation or ending of an English word you can make it Spanish - confirm to confirmar. However there are words that it is dangerous to do this with and they are in this book. - campo is a field or bit of country, not camping. Michel Thomas's audio course is very good. ISBN 0-340-78067-3

Mar de Piedra -Sea of Stone.
El Teatro - The Theatre.
Cara del Hombre - Face of the Man.
El Perro - The Dog. (perro is also 'but'.)
El Cocodrillo y El Elefante - The Crocodile and the Elephant.

Think of almost any western and you'll pick up quite a lot of simple spanish...
Por favor - please (the 'v' in spanish is like a soft 'b').
Gracias - thank you.
Hola - hello and Buenos dias - good morning are common greetings.
Sí- yes, No - no.
Ahora mismo - Right now.
Para mi - For me.
Cacho - a little bite to eat.
Camino – road/track/trail, also in the sense of a journey to be or being made.
Carretera is a tarred road.
Mucho viento - much wind.
Y ahora llueve - and now it is raining.
De aquí para alli - From here to there.
Dos cabezas - two heads.
Paseo - the ritual evening stroll.
A la próxima vez en España! - To the next time in Spain!
Hasta luego – till later (the next time we meet).
¿cuando ?- when.
La cuenta - the bill.
Tiene - do you have?
¿Dónde? - where?
Lo siento - I'm sorry.

I make up 'manglish' phrases that are not correct but generally are accepted and appreciated. I find it better to build a vocabulary of objects etc and string them together as need be than concentrate on grammar and tense. If you make it plain you are trying hard, and are apologetic about your lack of the language, then most Spanish will make an extra effort to understand you and speak simply in return. A corollary of this is that if you learn a few phrases perfectly and use them people will think your Spanish is good and reply fast and at length, at which point you become completely lost!
"Lo siento mi español es poco." When struggling to ask for something.

Cabrón - is a he-goat, don't use it where it could be taken as a reference to a man nearby as you may well end up in a fight - it is very rude! Joder and coño are not polite words, 'mear' is pissing and is very vulgar. Cojones (balls) is again very vulgar

To my father David Fred Gough who gave me through many ways, my interest in ideas and sketching as much else.
Oil paintings in the book are his.

To Stanley Gough his brother from whom came a bequest that allowed me to publish this book.

To my mother Hilary Gough for bequeathing me a practical side and who has been a tireless editor and without whose diligence there would be more questionable grammar and typos.

To Lucy my wife for all her support.

Thanks to:
Pete Creech, Editor of 'Gambalunga' the magazine of the Moto Guzzi Club of Great Britain, where the trips were published as articles and from where came the encouragement that led to further writing and my attempts to develop my style and to widen the themes of my writing.

To all my friends in Spain and to those who have been my travelling companions.

Thanks to Charlie Bielby for the photos (the ones with me in!) in Senorita Doradita.

Feel free to contact me with comments and questions - dunecangough@googlemail.com and visit my website (that is always needing work on it) - www.duncang.net